The Emergence of Total War

CIVIL WAR CAMPAIGNS AND COMMANDERS SERIES

Under the General Editorship of Grady McWhiney

PUBLISHED

Battle in the Wilderness: Grant Meets Lee by Grady McWhiney
Death in September: The Antietam Campaign
      by Perry D. Jamieson
Texans in the Confederate Cavalry by Anne J. Bailey
Sam Bell Maxey and the Confederate Indians by John C. Waugh
The Saltville Massacre by Thomas D. Mays
General James Longstreet in the West: A Monumental Failure
      by Judith Lee Hallock
The Battle of the Crater by Jeff Kinard
Cottonclads! The Battle of Galveston and the Defense of the
      Texas Coast by Donald S. Frazier
A Deep Steady Thunder: The Battle of Chickamauga
      by Steven E. Woodworth
The Texas Overland Expedition of 1863 by Richard Lowe
Raphael Semmes and the Alabama by Spencer C. Tucker
War in the West: Pea Ridge and Prairie Grove by William L. Shea
The Emergence of Total War by Daniel E. Sutherland
Iron and Heavy Guns: Duel Between the Monitor and Merrimac
      by Gene A. Smith

The Emergence of Total War

Daniel E. Sutherland

Under the General Editorship of Grady McWhiney

McWHINEY
FOUNDATION
PRESS

McMURRY UNIVERSITY
ABILENE, TEXAS

Cataloging-in-Publication Data

Sutherland, Daniel E.
    The emergence of total war / Daniel E. Sutherland.
       p. cm. – (Civil War campaigns and commanders)
    Includes bibliographical references and index.
    ISBN 1-886661-13-8 (pbk)

    1. Bull Run, 2nd Battle of , Va., 1862. 2. Virginia–History –Civil
War, 1861-1865–Campaigns. 3. United States–History–Civil War,
1861-1865–Campaigns. 4. Pope, John, 1822-1892. I. Title,

    E473.77.S88 1996
    973.7'32—dc20   96–24885
                                              CIP

Copyright ©1998, MCWHINEY FOUNDATION PRESS

All Rights Reserved

**McMurry Station, Box 637
Abilene, TX 79697-0637**

Printed in the United States of America

ISBN 1-886661-13-8

10 9 8 7 6 5 4 3 2 1

Book Designed by Rosenbohm Design Group

All inquiries regarding volume purchases of this book should be addressed to
MCWHINEY FOUNDATION PRESS, McMurry Station, Box 637, Abilene, TX 79697-0637.
Telephone inquiries may be made by calling (915) 691-6681.

A Note on the Series

Few segments of America's past excite more interest than Civil War battles and leaders. This ongoing series of brief, lively, and authoritative books–*Civil War Campaigns and Commanders*–salutes this passion with inexpensive and accurate accounts that are readable in a sitting. Each volume, separate and complete in itself, nevertheless conveys the agony, glory, death, and wreckage that defined America's greatest tragedy.

In this series, designed for Civil War enthusiasts as well as the newly recruited, emphasis is on telling good stories. Photographs and biographical sketches enhance the narrative of each book, and maps depict events as they happened. Sound history is meshed with the dramatic in a format that is just lengthy enough to inform and yet satisfy.

Grady McWhiney
General Editor

CONTENTS

1. A New Strategy   13

2. Devastation   23

3. Jackson and Pope at Cedar Mountain   33

4. Lee's Counterattack   50

5. Manassas, Again   65

6. End of the Miscreant   77

Epilogue   88

Appendix A: Battle of Cedar Mountain,
Confederate and Union Forces   92

Appendix B: Battle of Second Manassas,
Confederate and Union Forces   99

Further Reading   120

Index   124

The brief biographies accompanying the photographs
were written by Grady McWhiney and David Coffey.

CAMPAIGNS AND COMMANDERS SERIES

Map Key

Geography

 Trees

 Marsh

 Fields

Strategic Elevations

Rivers

Tactical Elevations

)|(Fords

 Orchards

—·—·—·— Political Boundaries

Human Construction

 Bridges

+-+-+-+-+-+-+ Railroads

Tactical Towns

● ○ Strategic Towns

□ ■ Buildings

‡ Church

✕ Roads

Military

 Union Infantry

 Confederate Infantry

 Cavalry

ılı Artillery

Headquarters

Encampments

Fortifications

Permanant Works

Hasty Works

Obstructions

 Engagements

 Warships

 Gunboats

 Casemate Ironclad

 Monitor

 Tactical Movements

 Strategic Movements

*Maps by
Donald S. Frazier, Ph.D.
Abilene, Texas*

MAPS

North Central Virginia   24

Afternoon at Cedar Mountain   44

Position of the Armies   62

Second Manassas, Evening of August 28   70

Second Manassas, Late Morning, August 29   74

Second Manassas, Late Afternoon, August 29   83

PHOTOGRAPHS AND ILLUSTRATIONS

Abraham Lincoln	15
Henry W. Halleck	16
John Pope	18
Black refugees fleeing with Pope's army	27
Street scene, Culpeper Court House	28
Thomas J. Jackson	30
Ambrose Powell Hill	32
Richard S. Ewell	34
Nathaniel P. Banks	35
Franz Sigel	36
Jubal A. Early	38
View of the Battle of Cedar Mountain	40
William B. Taliaferro	41
Samuel W. Crawford	42
Alpheus S. Williams	43
Robert Gould Shaw	46
Dead horses on Cedar Mountain battlefield	51
James E. B. Stuart	52
Clarissa Harlowe Barton	54
Robert E. Lee	56
James Longstreet	58
Philip Kearny	68
Rufus King	69
Isaac R. Trimble	72
Fitz John Porter	78
John Bell Hood	82

The Emergence of Total War

1
A NEW STRATEGY

The summer of 1862 shines as one of the bright moments in the history of the Confederacy. The Rebels had taken a pounding in the West that spring. Bloody Shiloh, the capture of New Orleans, the loss of Memphis, and the hasty evacuation of northern Mississippi had shocked soldiers and civilians from one end of the Confederacy to the other. With General George B. McClellan moving up the Peninsula toward Richmond, Abraham Lincoln hoped to deliver a knockout punch by ordering General John Pope to invade central Virginia. Together, Lincoln and Pope would implement a primitive version of what would later be called "total war." The phrase has come to mean many things, especially in light of the trench warfare of World War I and the unrestricted war waged against Germany and Japan in the 1940s. Still, Lincoln's plan not only to whip the Confederate army but to exhaust Rebel resources and destroy civilian morale grasped the essential elements of the strategy. His plan failed in 1862 when General Robert E. Lee drove McClellan off the Peninsula and then joined General Thomas J. "Stonewall" Jackson to shove Pope back to the defenses of Washington. By September, the game seemed to have turned, and so it had, at least for the moment.

In early June 1862, despite dramatic Federal victories in the West and Trans-Mississippi, Lincoln and the Union were in trouble. After launching his much-ballyhooed Peninsula Campaign, McClellan had been stopped cold by General Joseph E. Johnston at Seven Pines and Fair Oaks. Little Mac, in whom Lincoln had placed so much trust, had failed to win the Eastern victory the president hungered for so much. The Northern press grumbled about another missed opportunity. So did Radical Republicans, who had begun to attack Lincoln on two fronts. First, they demanded a more forceful prosecution of the war. It had become clear, they said, that the Rebels would not reenter the Union until they had been crushed militarily. They wanted no more "kid-glove warfare." Second, the Radicals saw this as an ideal time to press for emancipation and the introduction of black troops into Federal ranks.

Lincoln had long opposed both of the latter actions, but he suddenly found himself in a very vulnerable position. Both measures might be forced upon him by Congress unless he demonstrated that his war policies could work. In mid-July, he decided to compromise, thus buying time until he could launch a more aggressive military campaign against the South and show the Northern public and the politicians that he meant business. He told Secretary of State William Seward and Secretary of the Navy Gideon Welles that he had decided to emancipate *Rebel* slaves—that is, slaves in states that remained in rebellion—at an appropriate time. Indeed, recorded Welles in his secret diary, the president suddenly considered emancipation "a military necessity absolutely essential for the salvation of the Union." Lincoln also compromised on the use of black troops by announcing that he was "not unwill-

ing that commanders should, at their discretion, arm, for pure-
ly defensive purposes, slaves coming within the lines."

Equally important, Lincoln devised a new military strategy.
The president had come to realize that he was waging a war
unlike any previous one. Most wars had been won by annihilat-
ing the enemy's army, but it had become apparent after more
than a year of fighting that neither North nor South could man-
age such a feat. The rival armies were too large, too mobile,
and too dispersed to succumb to brute force. Then, too, there
was the Confederacy's civilian population. It remained
undaunted, defiant, and at once a goad and a comfort to its
fighting men. Lincoln believed the North must defeat both
Confederate civilians and soldiers before it could claim victory.

To achieve his goal, Lincoln would need a new army and
new generals. The new army would be christened the Army of
Virginia, its mission being to wreak havoc in the very center of

Abraham Lincoln: born Kentucky 1809; received little formal education; family
moved to Illinois where he held various clerking jobs; studied law; served in state
legislature as a Whig; settled in Springfield, practiced law, and in 1842 married
Mary Todd; retired from public
life after one term in U.S.
Congress, 1847–49; joined
Republican party in 1856 and
entered the growing debate over
sectionalism; in 1858 beaten for
U.S. Senate by Stephen A.
Douglas, but emerged from their
famous debate a national figure;
nominated by Republicans and
elected president in 1860; determined to preserve Union; issued
Emancipation Proclamation after
Union victory at Antietam in 1862;
reelected in 1864; mortally
wounded by John Wilkes Booth
14 April 1865; died the next day.

the Confederacy's capital state. Looking westward, he saw generals like Ulysses S. Grant, Henry W. Halleck, and John Pope pummeling the Rebels and gobbling up large pieces of territory. He, therefore, summoned Western generals to come East and perform their magic. First, in late June, he gave John Pope command of the new army and direction of the new strategy. For the moment, the components of Pope's army, which included three corps of 44,500 infantry plus 5,000 cavalry, were scattered between the Shenandoah Valley and Washington, D.C. The general's first job would be to assemble the parts. A few weeks later, Lincoln brought Halleck to Washington to serve him as general in chief, a post from which McClellan had been dismissed the previous March.

The forty-seven-year-old Halleck had graduated third in his class at West Point in 1839. Known in the army as "Old

Henry W. Halleck: born New York 1815; Halleck was graduated from the U.S. Military Academy in 1839, third in his class of thirty-one; commissioned a 2d lieutenant of engineers, he worked on New York Harbor's fortifications and made an

inspection tour of France; promoted to 1st lieutenant, he served in California during the Mexican War, earning a brevet to captain; an astute military thinker, "Old Brains," as he was called, authored *Report on the Means of National Defense* and *Elements of Military Art and Science*; he also translated Henri Jomini's *Vie Politique et Militaire de Napoleon*; promoted to the full rank of captain in 1853, Halleck resigned his commission the following year; he entered a lucrative legal practice in San Francisco, wrote two volumes on mining law, helped draft California's constitution, and was active in the state militia; with the onset of the Civil War, General Winfield Scott recommended Halleck to President Abraham Lincoln; commissioned directly into the regular army as a major general, Halleck became the fourth ranking officer in the army, following Scott, George B. McClellan, and John C.

Brains," he had written a textbook on international law and a tactical manual. As a theater commander in the West, he had received credit for the victories of others, even though his own credentials in the field, most notably his advance into Mississippi following the battle of Shiloh, lacked luster. But he had earned a reputation as a strategist and had waged a tough campaign against guerrillas in Missouri. Everyone to whom Lincoln spoke, including the venerable General Winfield Scott, said Halleck was the man. Pope, too, who had been something of a Halleck protege, recommended him.

But Pope was the key. Born March 16, 1822, in Louisville, Kentucky, Pope was the son of a territorial and Federal judge, nephew of a U.S. senator, and connected by marriage to Mary Todd Lincoln's family. He graduated from West Point in 1842 as one of a class that would provide seventeen generals to U.S.

Frémont; always an effective administrator, Halleck took command of the Department of the Missouri in November 1861, succeeding Frémont, and brought much-needed order to the chaotic West; in March his command was extended and redesignated the Department of the Mississippi; much of his department's success came with the battlefield accomplishments of his subordinates, Generals U.S. Grant (Forts Henry and Donelson, Shiloh), Samuel Curtis (Pea Ridge), and John Pope (Island No. 10); Halleck, however, proved an inept field commander when, after Shiloh, he took control of Grant's army and failed to crush the badly outnumbered Rebels at Corinth; named commander in chief of U.S. forces, Halleck moved to Washington, D.C., where his role became increasingly advisory and administrative; displaced by Grant's promotion in March 1864, Halleck became chief of staff and served credibly for the balance of the war; afterward, he headed the Military Division of the James, from April to June 1865, and the Division of the Pacific until 1869, when he assumed command of the Division of the South, headquartered at Louisville, Kentucky; he died there in 1872. General Halleck was extremely unpopular among his fellow officers and members of the Lincoln Administration; he owned a poor disposition, was difficult to work with, and frequently criticized other generals; this, combined with poor leadership qualities and his demonstrated inability as a field commander, left him the target of much ridicule; but he was a fine administrator and as such contributed greatly to the Federal victory and was especially useful after Grant became commanding general.

John Pope: born Kentucky 1822; Pope was graduated from the U.S. Military Academy in 1842, seventeenth in his class of fifty-six; commissioned a 2d lieutenant in the Topographical Engineers, he spent four years on survey duty and earned two brevets for gallantry during the Mexican War; promoted to 1st lieutenant he resumed engineering activities on the frontier and was elevated to captain in 1856; following the outbreak of the Civil war, Pope was commissioned a brigadier general in the volunteer army in June 1861; after various district and field assignments in Missouri, he assumed command of the Army of the Mississippi,

with which he captured New Madrid and Island No.10 on the Mississippi, opening the northern approaches to Memphis; in March 1862 he was promoted to major general of volunteers; ordered to the East by President Abraham Lincoln to impart the lessons of Western victory to the struggling Federal armies in Virginia, Pope had the poor judgement to say as much in addresses to his new command; his vainglorious pronouncements angered the Eastern soldiers, while his threatened severe treatment of Confederate sympathizers in Federal-occupied Virginia earned him the wrath of Robert E. Lee, who termed him a miscreant in his only such reaction to an opposing commander; to emphasize his new stature, Pope was awarded the regular army rank of brigadier general in July 1862, but quickly proved to be anything but the savior Lincoln had hoped for; thoroughly outgeneraled by Lee, Pope and his Army of Virginia were routed at Second Bull Run in August; although he attempted to pass blame for the defeat to his subordinates, and succeeded in having General Fitz John Porter cashiered from the army, Pope was relieved of command days after the battle; reassigned to command the distant Department of the Northwest, he was in effect removed from the war; he performed ably in his new role, most notably in suppressing the Sioux uprising in Minnesota; brevetted major general, U.S.A, he was mustered out of the volunteer army in September 1866; he held various departmental commands in the postwar army and proved to be an effective administrator during the Indian Wars; promoted to the full rank of major general in 1882, he retired as commander of the Military Division of the Pacific in 1886; General Pope died at Sandusky, Ohio, in 1892.

and C.S. armies. He had won a brevet captaincy in the Mexican War and gained permanent promotion to captain in 1856 for his service with the topographical engineers. His experience and family connections produced a general's star in June 1861. He added a second star for capturing New Madrid, Missouri, and the Confederate-held Island No. 10 in the Mississippi River as part of a series of well-executed movements in March and April 1862 with the Army of Mississippi. Personally, Pope was a self-confident braggart, who could be terribly offensive and abrasive. "Although he was brave, clever, and educated," admitted one observer, "he inspired distrust by his much promising and general love of gossip." More harshly, a fellow officer once said, "I don't care for John Pope one pinch of owl dung."

Yet Pope had demonstrated with his service in Missouri that he could fight the sort of war Lincoln wanted. In the summer of 1861, Pope was thrown into the cauldron of guerrilla warfare in Missouri. Like several other Federal generals in the Trans-Mississippi, including Halleck, John Frémont, and William T. Sherman, Pope reacted forcefully to the threat of bushwhackers and saboteurs. To control the region, Federal officers routinely issued orders that levied harsh fines, suppressed unlawful assemblies, arrested men bearing arms, and confiscated the property of civilians who engaged in partisan warfare or harbored guerrillas.

In August 1861, the 16th Illinois Infantry had been fired on as it passed by rail at Palmyra and Hunnewell, Missouri. One man was killed and another wounded. Two days later, Pope issued a proclamation: "If the guilty persons are not delivered up as required,....the whole brigade will be moved into your county, and contributions levied to the amount of $10,000 on Marion County and $5,000 on the city of Palmyra." That same summer, Pope issued a more sweeping proclamation for all of northern Missouri in which he charged communities to police themselves and ensure that Federal soldiers and property went unharmed: "If the people of the counties are not willing or able to enforce the peace among themselves, and to prevent the organizing of companies to make war on the United States, the military force will perform the service, but the expenses must be paid by the county in which such service is necessary." Within weeks, he reported that his policies had been completely successful in preventing further attacks and destruction.

Lincoln had been uneasy about his army's response to guerrillas and its relations with civilians in the Trans-Mississippi. Missouri, after all, was still in the Union, and Lincoln was determined to stay on good terms with the inhabitants. He recognized that Missouri was a chaotic place, and efforts there to establish martial law could follow no uniform or coherent policy. Military directives must necessarily be issued on local initiative. Yet Lincoln still hoped in those early months of the war to pursue a conciliatory policy toward the Rebels, in the belief that the South's latent unionism might still emerge and peace be restored. So when John Frémont threatened to go too far by emancipating Missouri slaves in 1861, Lincoln had reprimanded him and eventually removed him from command. Now, many months later, the situation had changed. Such measures no longer seemed unreasonable.

Beyond his military credentials, connections to the Todd family, and reputation as a man of action, Pope appealed to Lincoln in other ways. Lincoln had practiced law before Pope's father, and all the Popes, including Pope's father-in-law (a congressman from Ohio) were staunch Republicans. Lincoln knew Pope personally, and had even made him part of his entourage in traveling from Springfield, Illinois, to Washington for his presidential inauguration. Now, at this critical juncture in the war, Lincoln found himself in a tight military and political situation. He needed advice from proven leaders and men he could trust. He believed Pope qualified on both counts.

Within days of Pope's arrival at the capital, the Eastern military situation had reached a crisis. McClellan, once more leading his massive Army of the Potomac toward Richmond, had been stopped again, this time by Robert E. Lee in the Seven Days' Battles, and with even more disastrous results than in his earlier skirmish against Johnston. The Chicago *Tribune* called it a "stunning disaster." Lincoln called it unfair. It was "unreasonable," he told a political friend in contrasting the Western and Eastern theaters, "that a series of successes, extending through half-a-year, and clearing more than a thousand square miles of country, should help us so little, while a single half-defeat should hurt us so much."

Seeing that control of the West would mean nothing unless his new army and new commander produced results, Lincoln turned Pope loose and told him to win victories. The general began to concentrate his army in north-central Virginia during the first half of July. He ordered General Franz Sigel's Corps of 11,500 men to march from the Shenandoah Valley to Sperryville. General Nathaniel P. Banks would move his corps of 14,500 from the Valley to Little Washington, a few miles northeast of Sperryville. A division from General Irvin McDowell's Corps stationed at Manassas was shifted to the Rappahannock River below Warrenton. Pope left a second of McDowell's infantry divisions at Fredericksburg, but he ordered the cavalry brigade of General John P. Hatch to Culpeper, where he planned eventually to rendezvous his entire command.

On July 14, Pope issued a notorious proclamation to his new Eastern army: "I have come to you from the West, where we have always seen the back of our enemies; from an army whose business it has been to seek the adversary and to beat him when he was found; whose policy has been attack and not defense." By late July, Pope had also issued four general orders (Nos. 5, 7, 11, 13) to neutralize Virginia's civilian population as a factor in the war, and to show his army, the president, and the Confederacy that absolutely nothing would stand between him and total victory.

The Army of Virginia, announced Pope, would "subsist upon the country." Civilians would be "held responsible" for any disruption of Union supply or communication lines and attacks on army personnel. Whenever a railroad line, wagon road, or telegraph was sabotaged, all civilians within a five-mile radius would be "turned out in mass" to repair the damage. Citizens caught firing on soldiers would be punished in a variety of ways, from having their homes "razed to the ground" to paying an indemnity. In either case, perpetrators would be "shot, without awaiting civil process." Southerners unwilling to take the oath of allegiance would be turned out of their homes and sent behind Rebel lines. Anyone attempting to return within Federal lines would be shot.

Lincoln and Secretary of War Edwin Stanton approved all of it. In mid-July, receiving complaints that General John Phelps, military governor of Arkansas and Louisiana, had threatened to emancipate slaves in his department, Lincoln responded that it was the fault of the people of Louisiana, not his own, that they were "annoyed by the presence of General Phelps." He continued: "I am a patient man—always willing to forgive on the Christian terms of repentance; and also to give ample time for repentance. Still, I must save the government if possible…. [And] it may as well be understood, once for all, that I shall not surrender this game leaving any available card unplayed." A few days later, Lincoln issued an executive order that permitted Union field commanders "to seize and use any property, real and personal," that could serve the military effort, and to destroy civilian property "for proper military objects."

2
DEVASTATION

The impact of the Pope-Lincoln policy became immediately apparent in the destruction of property and intimidation of the people in north-central Virginia. One Union officer reported: "Our men now believe they have a perfect right to rob, tyrannize, threaten & maltreat any one they please, under the Orders of Gen Pope." The orders also changed men's opinion of Pope. They had made sport of his bombastic July 14 address and a widely quoted remark that he liked to maintain his "headquarters in the saddle." The latter seemed a rather empty boast for a man who sat behind a desk in Washington, and it inspired the nearly inevitable rejoinder that Pope's saddle, if ever he occupied it, would be better suited to his "hindquarters." But the orders ended much of the jesting. Soldiers and politicians exulted over a policy that had apparently "infused new vigor" and "additional strength and courage" into the army. "There has never been such universal

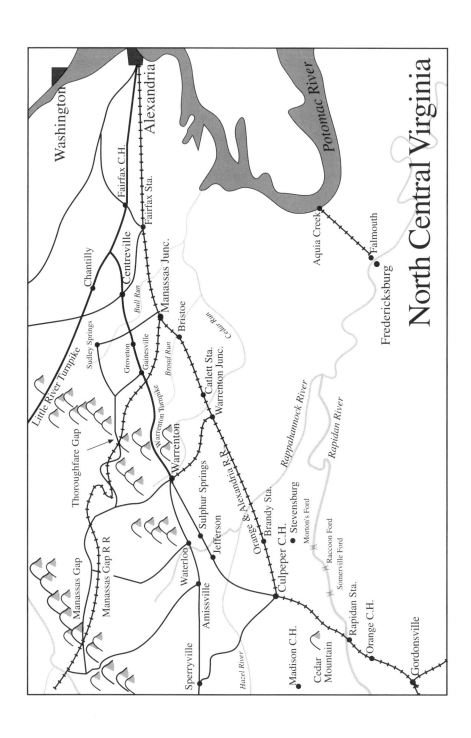

North Central Virginia

good feeling in any army with which I have been as is manifest here now to see the government take strong measures," one enthusiastic soldier informed his wife. "No victory we have gained has been worth as much to the army in the field and the nation's prospects as this order."

Meanwhile, confiscation, destruction of property, and intimidation became the order of the day in Union-occupied Virginia. Federal officers were supposed to supervise confiscation and issue vouchers specifying the type, amount, and value of goods taken; but many soldiers, sensing a license in Pope's orders that probably had not been intended, seized whatever took their fancy. Pope's orders had "produced a decided revolution in the feelings and practices of the soldiery," confirmed one Northerner. "Men who at home would have shuddered at the suggestion of touching another's property," he observed in only mild reproach, "now appropriate whatever comes in their reach." "Straggling soldiers have been known to rob the farm houses and even small cottages, the homes of the poor, of every ounce of food or forage found in them," declared a lieutenant in Pope's army. People safe in their homes, far removed from the swath of war, could not imagine, he lamented, the brutality and suffering in this part of Virginia. "Families have been left without the means of preparing a meal of victuals." What is more, he added bitterly, "The villains urge as authority, 'General Pope's order.'"

Yet confiscation was far from being the worst plague to strike Virginia. "In every direction there appeared a frightful scene of devastation," reported a member of the 1st New Jersey Cavalry as he surveyed the work of fellow soldiers in Culpeper County, the worst-hit region. "Furniture, valuable in itself and utterly useless to them, was mutilated and defaced; beds were defiled and cut to pieces; pictures and mirrors were slashed with sabres or perforated by bullets; windows were broken, doors torn from their hinges, houses and barns burned down." At Berry Hill plantation, soldiers stole all of Lucy

Thom's clothes, and she watched helplessly as they carried her melodeon to the slave quarters, destroyed all her corn, and took away her horses. After ransacking one minister's house, soldiers proceeded to wreck his church by order of their officers. Soldiers burned the house and out buildings of a Confederate army captain besides rounding up his slaves, confiscating his livestock, and laying waste to "his entire farm."

The Federals seemed intent on breaking Rebel spirits by whatever means came to hand. Families, even poor families, had food "wantonly snatched from their mouths and wasted by brutal men." Union cavalrymen terrorized two sisters who lived below the Rappahannock River. The rowdies galloped up to the house and demanded to know the whereabouts of the married sister's husband. The women swore that he was not there, but this only seemed to enrage the Yankees. They dismounted and cursed the woman as they approached the house with "pistols in hand, sabers clanking, spurs rattling." If they caught the miserable son-of-a-bitch, growled one man, they would hang him in his own front yard. "No," his partner interrupted gleefully, "we will scalp his damn old bald head just here at the door." Laughing, they proceeded to sack the house and carry away what they pleased. The sisters thanked God that the men rode off without having treated their persons in similar fashion.

Unprotected women invited the worst behavior, for "insult and outrage ever walk hand-in-hand with plunder." "Instances are reported," lamented one observer, "of deeds of violence perpetrated upon respectable ladies...which are without a parallel, save in the annals of the infamous Yankee race." People were too discreet to mention the victims' names or to dwell on the "repulsive details" of the attacks, but all felt sickened by the acts. "The Yankee rule in the county is severe beyond precedent in the war," reported a Virginian of Culpeper. "The most abominable outrages are being reported on the females, white and black." A British journalist confirmed that the war in all north-central Virginia was being waged "in a way that cast mankind two centuries back toward barbarism."

Black Virginians, slave and free, received mixed treatment. Pope's invasion gave slaves in the vicinity their first good opportunity to escape bondage. Large numbers of blacks who had been placed in county jails by their masters, preparatory to being sent to Richmond for safekeeping, were released by the Federals. Elsewhere, slaves who had not already been spirited away to safe havens delighted to see so many blue uniforms. They gazed with "wonder and joy upon the banner of the free," and the Federals, who regarded their actions as a form of revenge against Virginia slaveowners, took especial pleasure in urging slaves to leave their masters. Particularly bold female slaves smacked the faces of their mistresses as they exited, and it was "not an uncommon thing for them to dress in their mistresses' clothes [and] put on their jewelry and ornaments," reported an observer. Another favorite

Black refugees take advantage of John Pope's occupation to leave Culpeper. The Rappahannock railroad bridge stands in the background.

departing gesture was to "play the Piano for the 'Northern gemmen'" before setting out on the road to freedom.

Pope's men did not execute or banish anyone, as they had been licensed to do, but they did arrest a good many civilians. "Every man of prominence who has come in their [Federals'] way has been arrested and sent off to Washington," reported one resident, "their personal goods stolen or destroyed, their stock butchered, and their lands laid waste." They incarcerated one young woman "for resenting with becoming spine" the coarse insults of a Union soldier. Another "young and lovely lady" was thrown into jail because she drew a pistol on a soldier who had entered her house and "grossly and brutaly insulted" her. Soldiers dragged an elderly Episcopal minister from his church in Culpeper and sent him to Washington because he dared lead his congregation in prayer "for the welfare of the Southern Confederacy and the success of its arms."

The intimidation and arrests soon took effect, as the Federals thoroughly cowed most of the population. "A town so

Street scene, Culpeper Court House. The building with the weather vane is the court house. The streets were typically deserted during John Pope's occupation in August 1862.

sombre as Culpeper I have never known," reported a journalist accompanying the army to Culpeper Court House. "The shutters were closed in the shop windows, the dwellings seemed tenantless, no citizens were abroad." Shortages of food and high prices for what remained were reported everywhere. "Absolute starvation" reigned in some quarters, and "pinched, pining faces" betrayed a ravaged population. Even the dogs were "skinny and savage for want of sustenance." A few people responded by reporting meekly to the provost marshal's office, where they asked to take the "exorable oath" in order to save self and property. A larger, only slightly bolder, number refused to swear allegiance to the United States, but they did promise not to interfere with Federal troops.

Still, Virginia's Rebels were far from subdued. People displayed their defiance in different ways, but the general air of hostility toward the Federals was marked. "Secession is more rabid and bitter here than in any other place we have been in Virginia," swore a Federal cavalryman in Culpeper. "The men generally retain a sullen silence while the women wear a contemptuous and disdainful Sneer." The four tempestuous daughters of a local hotel proprietor scorned Union officers who roomed with them. When dining, they made a show of sitting apart from the officers and speaking disparagingly of "Yankees." When promenading through town, dressed in their finest crinolines, the sisters refused to acknowledge the existence of any Federal they passed, and they relished any opportunity to scorn with a "pert flourish" symbols of Federal authority, particularly the national flag.

More aggressively, physical harassment of Union troops continued. The army, as one perceptive invader appreciated, was "surrounded by secessionists, and watched by spies calling themselves 'Union men.'" Amateur saboteurs attempted to derail supply trains and cut telegraph wires. Some citizens took to the woods to plague detachments of Federal troops as guerrillas. The staccato exchange of pistol and rifle fire vibrated across the region. "A man was shot a few minutes [ago] down to the creek bathing by some bushwhacker," a Federal informed his wife. Even as he wrote, an officer was dispatched to arrest several suspects.

People made so bold, in part, because they heard rumors that Stonewall Jackson was rushing to the rescue. Lee and the Confederate government were outraged by Pope's orders and the actions of his men. President Jefferson Davis quickly announced that if any Southern civilians were murdered or executed, an equal number of Pope's officers, if captured, would be hanged. A Richmond newspaper, describing Pope as "a compound of vulgar self-conceit, impudence and brutality," demanded that he be captured and executed. With McClellan contained south of Richmond following the Seven Days' Battles, Lee felt secure enough in his defense of the capital to dispatch Jackson and two divisions toward Culpeper. Soon

Thomas J. Jackson: born Virginia 1824; graduated seventeenth of fifty-nine cadets in his 1846 class at the U.S. Military Academy; appointed 2d lieutenant in 3rd Artillery; participated in War with Mexico in 1847; brevetted captain for gallantry at Contreras and Churubusco and major for his conduct at Chapultepec; resigned from the U.S. Army in 1852 to accept a professorship of artillery tactics and optics at the Virginia Military Institute in Lexington, where he enforced rigid discipline,

expelled several cadets, and won the hatred of many others; students called him, behind his back: "Tom Fool," "Old Blue Light," "crazy as damnation," and "the worst teach that God ever made." Jackson's first wife, Elinor Junkin, died in childbirth; a later marriage to Mary Anna Morrison produced a daughter. In 1861 Jackson joined the Confederate army; appointed colonel and then brigadier general, he won his famous nickname "Stonewall" in July at the Battle of Manassas, where General Barnard E. Bee, observing the steadiness of Jackson's Virginians, shouted to his South Carolinians: "Look, men! There stands Jackson like a stone wall! Rally behind the Virginians!" Promoted to

after his arrival on July 19 at Gordonsville, a dozen miles south of Culpeper, Stonewall asked Lee for more men. Marse Robert responded near the end of the month by sending him General Ambrose Powell Hill's Division. Lee wanted Jackson to "destroy" the "miscreant," Pope.

As Jackson began a slow, methodical march toward the Rapidan River, he knew his men were primed and ready to wallop Pope. They had heard all about the ravaging of Culpeper. News of the "savage and barbarous treatment" dealt one farmer by "Lincoln's bandits" seemed to be typical. "They plundered him of all he had, his corn, wheat, and pork, killed his hogs, drove off his beef cattle and even his milch cows," said the report. "They even threatened to shoot this gentleman for having a loaded musket in his house." Jackson's men muttered that "the man with the movable headquarters had better commence moving."

major general, Jackson began in March 1862 his brilliant Shenandoah Valley Campaign; in June he shifted his army to assist Lee in the Seven Days' Battles near Richmond; in August he fought Federal forces at Cedar Mountain, Groveton, and Second Manassas; in September, during Lee's Maryland Campaign, he captured a large Union garrison at Harpers Ferry and then rejoined Lee's army for the Battle of Sharpsburg; promoted in October to lieutenant general and commanding half of Lee's forces, Jackson repulsed a major Federal assault in December at Fredericksburg. In May 1863 Jackson fought his last battle at Chancellorsville, where he made a spectacular flanking attack on the exposed Federal right flank and then rode out to locate the enemy's position; while returning in the darkness, he was mistaken for Federal cavalry and shot by his own troops. Jackson developed pneumonia and died on May 10, 1863. "I know not how to replace him," lamented Lee. "Without disparagement to others, it may be safely said he has become, in the estimation of the Confederacy, emphatically 'the hero of the war.' Around him clustered with peculiar warmth their gratitude, their affections, and their hopes," reported Secretary of War James A. Seddon. "Stonewall Jackson," as his most recent biographer observed, "ranks among the most brilliant commanders in American history. Even though his field service in the Civil War lasted but two years, his movements continued to be studied at every major military academy in the world."

Ambrose Powell Hill: born Virginia 1825; graduated fifteenth in the class of 1847 at the U.S. Military Academy; 2d lieutenant 1st Artillery in 1847 and served in Mexico, but saw no action; 1st lieutenant in 1851; participated in Florida Seminole campaigns; served in D.C. office of coast survey, 1855 to 1860; married Kitty Morgan McClung, sister of John Hunt Morgan, in 1859; resigned from U.S. Army in 1861; appointed colonel of 13th Virginia Infantry; in 1862 promoted to brigadier general; commanded brigade and won praise at Williamsburg; promoted to major general and given command of the Confederacy's largest division, which he led successfully but with heavy losses during the battles of the Seven Days; transferred after a disagreement with Longstreet to Stonewall Jackson's command, Hill received praise for his actions at Cedar Mountain and Second Manassas, yet enjoyed his greatest fame for saving the Army of Northern Virginia from defeat by his timely arrival on Lee's right flank at Sharpsburg; in December 1862 his actions at Fredericksburg heightened a controversy between Hill and Jackson that ended only with Stonewall's death following the Battle of Chancellorsville in May 1863;

promoted to lieutenant general and given command of the newly formed Third Corps in Lee's army, Hill opened the Battle of Gettysburg, but sickness limited his effectiveness; he repulsed Federals at Falling Waters, Maryland, on the retreat to Virginia, but suffered his worst defeat making a bold attack at Bristoe Station in October; in 1864 he fought in the Wilderness, but illness deprived him of command from May 8-21; participated in actions from the North Anna River to Cold Harbor, and in Lee's defense of Petersburg, where from June 1864 to March 1865 Hill met and defeated "every Federal effort to break Lee's right"; late in March he took sick-leave, his best biographer explains, suffering from kidney malfunctions that slowly produced uremia, the results of a gonorrhea infection contracted during a summer 1844 furlough from West Point; Hill returned to the front on April 2, 1865, where he was killed trying to reestablish his lines. Genial but quarrelsome, reckless and impetuous in battle, only five feet nine inches tall, and weighing just 145 pounds, "Little Powell" favored bright red shirts and enjoyed the confidence of his troops. "A more brilliant, useful soldier and chivalrous gentleman never adorned the Confederate army," said General William Mahone.

3

JACKSON AND POPE AT CEDAR MOUNTAIN

The two forces collided on August 9 in the shadow of Cedar Mountain, nearly eight miles southwest of Culpeper Court House. Jackson had pushed his 24,000 men across the Rapidan River on the night of August 8 and the morning of August 9. The Rebels moved sluggishly because Old Jack, as was his tendency, had not confided the complete plan of action to his three division commanders, A.P. Hill, General Richard S. Ewell, and General Charles S. Winder. Hill was furious, and a confrontation with Jackson left hard feelings between the two men for the remainder of Jackson's life.

Pope, anticipating a move against him, had further consolidated his three widely separated corps. He had with him at Culpeper Court House a portion of General Irvin McDowell's Corps (the remainder being at Fredericksburg, thirty-five miles

Richard S. Ewell: born D.C. (of Virginian stock) 1817; graduated U.S. Military Academy in 1840, thirteenth in his class; appointed 2d lieutenant in the 1st Dragoons; promoted to 1st lieutenant in 1845; served on the frontier; participated in the Mexican War; brevetted captain in 1847 for gallant conduct at Contreras and Churubusco; promoted to captain in 1849; won further distinction against the Apaches in New Mexico in 1857. Resigned from U.S. Army in 1861 to join the

Confederacy; appointed lieutenant colonel of cavalry and wounded at Fairfax Court House, Va., in June, he quickly advanced to brigadier general and command of a brigade at First Manassas; promoted to major general in 1862, Ewell led a division in the Shenandoah Valley under Stonewall Jackson's command at Winchester and Cross Keys; fought next at Gaines' Mill in defense of Richmond, and then during the Second Manassas Campaign at Cedar Mountain and Groveton, where he received a wound that cost him his left leg. Recuperated under the care of his first cousin, Lizinka Campbell Brown, whom he married in May 1863; promoted to lieutenant general and given command of a corps after Stonewall Jackson's death, Ewell defeated a large Federal force at Winchester, led the Army of Northern Virginia's advance into Pennsylvania, and launched an attack on the Federal right at Gettysburg, but failed to take Cemetery Ridge, for which he received considerable criticism. In 1864 he commanded his corps in the Wilderness and at Spotsylvania, but Ewell's broken health forced Lee to transfer him from corps command to responsibility for the defense of Richmond; in 1865, during the retreat toward Appomattox, Ewell commanded a mixed corps of soldiers, sailors, and marines; surrounded and forced to surrender at Sayler's Creek, he was imprisoned until summer; moved to his wife's plantation in Maury County, Tennessee, where he died of pneumonia on January 25, 1872, just five days after his wife succumbed to the same illness. Douglas S. Freeman described him as "bald, pop-eyed and long beaked, with a piping voice that seems to fit his appearance as a strange, unlovely bird"; his sharp tongue matched his fighting spirit, but the loss of his leg, headaches, indigestion, and sleeplessness drained both his energy and effectiveness. "A truer and nobler spirit never drew sword," proclaimed General Longstreet.

Nathaniel P. Banks: born Massachusetts 1816; received little formal education; admitted to the bar in 1839; entered Massachusetts legislature, rising to speaker of the house; presided over the state's 1853 Constitutional Convention and was elected to the U.S. House of Representatives that same year; speaker of the House 1856; elected governor of Massachusetts in 1858, serving until 1861; at the outbreak of the Civil War, he offered his services to the Union and was appointed major general U.S. Volunteers by President Abraham Lincoln; headed the Department of Annapolis before assuming command of the Department of the Shenandoah; prevented from reinforcing General G.B. McClellan on the Peninsula by the aggressive actions of General T.J. Jackson's Confederates in the Shenandoah Valley; defeated Jackson at Kernstown, Virginia, in March 1862, but fared poorly in subsequent actions; assigned to command the Second Corps in General John Pope's newly-formed Army of Virginia; defeated by Jackson at Cedar Mountain during the Second Bull Run Campaign in August 1862; after Pope's army was dismantled, Banks headed briefly the Military District of Washington before assuming command of the Department of the Gulf; conducted a costly operation against Port Hudson, which fell only after Vicksburg's capture left it untenable; directed the marginally successful Bayou Teche Expedition in the fall of 1863; following the failure of his Red River Expedition in 1864, Banks was relieved by General E.R.S. Canby; received thanks of Congress for Port Hudson; mustered out of volunteer service in 1865; returned to Congress where he served six more terms (not

consecutively); declining health forced his retirement from Congress in 1890; he died in Massachusetts in 1894. General Banks was among the most active of the higher-ranking "political" generals. He was consistently placed in command positions that were beyond his abilities; his personal courage, devotion, and tenacity could not overcome his lack of military training.

Franz Sigel: born Grand Duchy of Baden (Germany) 1824; he was graduated from the military academy at Karlsrule in 1843 and served as a lieutenant in the service of Grand Duke Leopold; his participation in the failed Revolution of 1848 caused him to flee Germany; after stays in Switzerland and England, Sigel made his way to the United States in 1852; settling in New York, he taught school and held a commission in the New York Militia; removing to St. Louis, Missouri, he became director of schools and a leader in the large German community there; at the outbreak of the Civil War he offered his services to the Union and was appointed colonel of the 3d Missouri Infantry and, shortly thereafter, brigadier general of volunteers; he participated in the capture of Camp Jackson and at Wilson's Creek in 1861; he

commanded a division and played a conspicuous role in the Battle of Pea Ridge in March 1862; promoted to major general, Sigel transferred to the Eastern Theater, where he led a division in the Shenandoah Valley; he commanded the First Corps, Army of Virginia, during the Second Bull Run Campaign of 1862; thereafter, he directed the Eleventh Corps, Army of the Potomac, from September 1862 through February 1863, but saw little action and was forced to relinquish corps command due to poor health; returning to duty in March 1864, he assumed command of the Department of West Virginia; in May Sigel's command was routed at New Market, Virginia, by General John C. Breckinridge's Confederate force that included a contingent of cadets from the Virginia Military Institute; relieved of departmental command, Sigel took charge of the Reserve Division, Department of West Virginia, but saw little action for the rest of the war; he resigned his commission in May 1865; after the war he became active in Democratic politics and ran for numerous offices, eventually becoming a U.S. pension agent in New York by appointment of President Grover Cleveland; he died at New York City in 1902. Although his New Market defeat destroyed his military reputation, General Sigel deserved much credit for rallying thousands of German immigrants to the Union cause; "I fights mit Sigel" became a proud exclamation of German-born soldiers throughout the Federal army.

to the east) and General Banks's full corps, which had rendezvoused from north of Culpeper on the night of August 8. General Sigel still lumbered southeastward with his corps from Sperryville, nearly thirty miles away. Potentially, Pope had at least twice as many men as Jackson.

Pope's men struck first, although that was not what he had intended. Pope had wanted only to block Jackson's advance, in hopes of avoiding a general engagement until his entire force had assembled. But with the division of General Christopher C. Augur commanding the northern edge of the battlefield—a broad plateau covered with unharvested cornfields between Cedar Mountain and the Culpeper Road—Nathaniel Banks wanted to avenge earlier defeats by Jackson in the Shenandoah Valley. Banks believed he outnumbered the Rebels, as indeed he did at this stage of the battle. Winder's and Hill's divisions were still strung out along the Culpeper Road to the rear of Ewell's advance. But as these additional units deployed, Banks would find himself with the smaller force.

Mounted and dismounted Federal skirmishers clashed at about 3 P.M. with the 13th Virginia Infantry, a goodly number of whom had been recruited from the vicinity. The 13th Virginia formed the spearhead of General Jubal A. Early's Brigade, part of Ewell's Corps, on the Confederate right. Deploying in front of them, forming the Federal left, were the three brigades of Augur's division, commanded by generals John W. Geary, Henry Prince, and George S. Greene. A few of Early's men fell wounded in the preliminary exchange of fire, but then men had been dropping all morning in the 100-degree temperatures of this August day. Many soldiers, especially the "stout" ones, fell out of ranks "utterly exhausted, some fainting, some victims of sun stroke, and many from sheer want of strength and will to go further."

At 3:30 P.M., the 13th Virginia, commanded by Colonel James A. Walker, fell back to a position on the brigade's left.

Artillery arrived. Early's Brigade pushed forward, across a road that led to the farmhouse of Catherine Crittenden, on the right, and to the crest of a small knoll. Ahead stretched the plain. At the opposite end, a thousand yards distant, Federal guns had already commenced firing. "We are in for it now," the Rebels whispered among themselves. Early placed two batteries in a clump of cedar trees a few yards ahead on his right. The artillery duel began as Confederate infantry dropped back a few steps to lie down behind the knoll, safe from Yankee guns.

At 4 P.M., Ewell arrived to take personal command of his division, and the battle began in earnest. He positioned General Winder's artillery to the right of the Culpeper Road and additional batteries near Reverend Philip Slaughter's

Jubal A. Early: born Virginia 1816; Early was graduated from the U.S. Military Academy in 1837, eighteenth in his class of fifty; commissioned into the artillery he served against the Seminoles in Florida before resigning to study law; he practiced law, served one term in the Virginia legislature, and acted as the state's attorney for Franklin County from 1842 to 1852; he also served in the Mexican War as a major of Virginia volunteers; during the Virginia convention of 1861, Early voted against secession but nonetheless offered his services to his native state; he was commissioned a colonel in the Virginia militia and entered Confederate service as colonel of the 24th Virginia; he led a brigade at First Manassas and was promoted to brigadier general in August 1861; wounded at Williamsburg the following spring, he returned to participate in the Seven Days' Battles; he commanded a brigade under General T.J. "Stonewall" Jackson in the Army of Northern Virginia at Second Manassas, Antietam, and Fredericksburg; promoted to major general in January 1863, he commanded a division at Chancellorsville, Gettysburg, and the Wilderness; after directing General A.P. Hill's Third Corps dur-

house on Cedar Mountain—also known, rather ominously, as Slaughter Mountain. General Winder soon joined his artillerymen, despite the fact that his surgeon had advised him not to take the field. He had been so sick that he had been traveling in an ambulance for much of the previous week. But Winder was a warhorse and an artillerist by trade, so he could not resist dismounting, stripping off his jacket, and helping to direct the fire of his batteries.

At 4:30 P.M., Winder was about to shout instructions to one of the gunners when a Federal shell screeched between the general's body and his upraised left arm. He was "fearfully mangled," his whole left side ripped apart, his chest shattered. Winder fell straight backward and lay "quivering on the ground." Lieutenant McHenry Howard, a staff officer, rushed to

ing the Spotsylvania Campaign in May 1864, he assumed command of General Richard Ewell's Second Corps; duly promoted to lieutenant general in May 1864, Early was dispatched with his corps to clear the Shenandoah Valley of Federals; he drove General David Hunter's Federal forces from the valley, won a battle at Monocacy, Maryland, and pushed to the outskirts of Washington, D.C., before Federal reinforcements secured the capital; after troops from Early's command burned Chambersburg, Pennsylvania, Federal commander General U.S. Grant sent General Philip Sheridan with a large army to the valley; in September and October 1864 Sheridan's superior force defeated Early at Winchester, Fisher's Hill, and Cedar Creek, where the Confederates almost achieved a stunning victory; Sheridan launched a campaign of destruction that laid waste to the Shenandoah Valley, for which Early received much of the blame; the remnants of Early's command remained in the valley until finally scattered at Waynesboro in March 1865; Early was relieved in late March, only days before General Robert E. Lee's surrender at Appomattox; despite his ultimate defeat, Early had created a considerable diversion in the valley and occupied thousands of Federal troops for most of a year; after the war, Early travelled to Mexico and then to Canada, devoting much of his time to his memoirs, before returning to Virginia in 1869; in 1877 he became commissioner of the Louisiana Lottery; he also wrote and lectured on the war and served as president of the Southern Historical Society; General Early died at Lynchburg in 1894. Dark, irascible, and impetuous, he was a solid officer, in whom Lee placed a great deal of confidence.

This view of the Battle of Cedar Mountain by northern artist Edwin Forbes shows the alignment of Federal batteries as Pope's army prepares to advance.

William B. Taliaferro: born Virginia 1822; from a prominent Virginia family, Taliaferro, was graduated from the College of William and Mary in 1841 and studied law at Harvard; he served as a captain in the 11th U.S. Infantry and was promoted to major in the 9th U.S. Infantry during the Mexican War; a Virginia legislator from 1850 to 1853, he rose to the rank of major general in the state militia; following Virginia's secession, he commanded state troops on the Peninsula and entered Confederate service as colonel of the 23d Virginia Infantry in the summer of 1861; serving in Western Virginia, he fought at Rich Mountain and Corrick's Ford; he commanded a brigade in General W.W. Loring's Army of the Northwest (Virginia) and sided with Loring in that general's dispute with General T.J. "Stonewall" Jackson; despite being immensely unpopular with his troops and many fellow officers, Taliaferro was promoted to

brigadier general in March 1862 and was assigned, over Jackson's objection, to head a brigade in Jackson's Shenandoah Valley command; he served throughout Jackson's Valley Campaign and during the Seven Days' Battles; in August he assumed command of Jackson's former division during the Battle of Cedar Mountain and led it at Second Manassas, where he was seriously wounded; returning to duty, he played a minor role in the December 1862 Battle of Fredericksburg; denied promotion to major general, he secured a transfer to General P.G.T. Beauregard's Department of South Carolina, Georgia, and Florida; in July 1863, Taliaferro commanded the successful defense of Battery Wagner, near Charleston, that featured a spirited but disastrous assault by the black soldiers of Colonel Robert Gould Shaw's 54th Massachusetts; thereafter Taliaferro held several district commands, assisted in the evacuation of Savannah, and commanded a division under General Joseph E. Johnston in North Carolina during the final months of the war; although occasionally identified as a major general he was never officially conferred that rank; after the war he practiced law, served in the Virginia legislature from 1874 to 1879 and on the boards of William and Mary and the Virginia Military Institute; General Taliaferro also sat as judge of Gloucester County, Virginia, from 1891 to 1897; he died there in 1898.

him and asked, "General, do you know me?" Winder shifted his eyes toward the officer and breathed, "Oh yes," but Howard could see the general was doomed. He spoke of his wife and children at home in Maryland. A chaplain arrived and asked him to lift up his heart to God. "I do," Winder replied mechanically and faintly, "I do lift it up to Him." An ambulance carried the general to a grove near a schoolhouse, where he died before the end of the day. Meanwhile, his artillery chief, Major Richard S. Andrews, was nearly disemboweled by an exploding shell.

Civilians living on or near the battlefield responded variously to the swelling crescendo of battle. Many people, both black and white, headed for the homes of friends and relatives outside the range of the guns. Others, fascinated by the martial scene, lingered. A crowd of slaves from nearby Forest Grove plantation climbed onto the roof of a shed to get a better view of the white man's battle. Thirteen-year-old William Nalle, whose father owned a grand brick house behind Federal lines, had been playing on the battlefield with several black and white friends earlier in the day. When the boys suddenly found

Samuel W. Crawford: born Pennsylvania 1829; after graduating from medical school University of Pennsylvania in 1851 took post in Southwest as assistant surgeon; in 1861 led a battery at Fort Sumter and made major 13th U.S. Infantry; in 1862 appointed brigadier general U.S. Volunteers; led a brigade at Winchester and Cedar Mountain; wounded at Antietam; in 1863 led a division at Gettysburg; in 1864 commanded a division and briefly the Fifth Corps during the Virginia campaigns; brevetted through major general in both U.S. and volunteer services; commissioned lieutenant colonel in 2d Infantry; after war served at various places in the South; promoted to colonel in 1869; retired in 1873 with the rank of brigadier general; died in Philadelphia in 1892.

themselves trapped between the advancing armies, they wasted little time in retreating to the Nalle house.

Command of Winder's Division fell to General William B. Taliaferro, who very soon faced a crisis. Shortly before 6 P.M., General Samuel W. Crawford's Union Brigade, part of General Alpheus Williams's Division on the Federal right, moved forward into a recently harvested wheatfield above the Culpeper Road, across from the action in the cornfields. Almost immedi-

Alpheus S. Williams: born Connecticut 1810; graduated Yale University; studied law and travelled extensively before establishing a law practice in Detroit; served as a volunteer officer in the Mexican War; brigadier general of Michigan state troops; at the onset of the Civil War received a commission to brigadier general U.S. Volunteers May 1861; led a division under General N.P. Banks in the Shenandoah Valley and at Cedar Mountain; commanded a division in the Second Corps Army of Virginia but not actively engaged at Second Bull Run; directed the First Division of the newly formed Twelfth Corps and saw heavy fighting at Antietam, temporarily heading the corps following the death J.K.F. Mansfield; ably led his division at Chancellorsville and Twenfth Corps at Gettysburg; sent West with the Eleventh and Twelfth Corps, not actively engaged at Chattanooga; when the Eleventh and Twelfth Corps were merged into the Twentieth Corps, Williams received the First Division; led his division, and frequently the corps throughout the Atlanta Campaign, General W.T. Sherman's "March to the Sea," and through the Carolinas; brevetted major general U.S. Volunteers for war service, he mustered out of the volunteer organization 1866; minister to El Salvador 1866–69; unsuccessfully ran for governor of Michigan 1870; elected to U.S. House of Representatives 1874 and re-elected 1876; died in office 1878. General Williams was among the most solid of non-professional or "political" generals. Although he frequently commanded a corps, he was apparently never considered for permanent corps command. He ended the war a very experienced brigadier and deserving of higher rank.

ately, Taliaferro's left flank and front were threatened by Crawford's advancing infantry. The Federals smashed through one gray-clad brigade above the road and moved obliquely against Taliaferro. Intense musketry caused disarray in Rebel ranks. The Confederates fell back.

At this critical moment in the battle, up galloped Jackson. Quickly grasping the situation, Stonewall turned Taliaferro's faltering men, many of whom had formed part of his old division and legendary Stonewall Brigade. Seeking to rally them, Jackson tried to draw his sword, something he had never done in battle, but found the blade rusted tight in its scabbard.

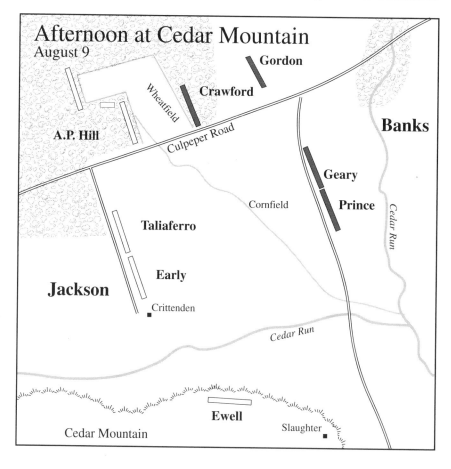

Afternoon at Cedar Mountain
August 9

Gordon

Crawford

Wheatfield

Banks

A.P. Hill

Culpeper Road

Geary

Cornfield

Prince

Cedar Run

Taliaferro

Early

Jackson

Crittenden

Cedar Run

Ewell

Cedar Mountain

Slaughter

Unperturbed, Stonewall released the scabbard from his belt and waved the whole affair high above his head. He lurched forward on Old Sorrel and cried out above the roar of battle, "Rally, brave men, and press forward!"

The retreating ranks gazed in wonder. Could it really be Old Jack? They had never seen him display such energy. He was seemingly transformed by combat, with the "light of battle" radiating from his blue eyes. "Your general will lead you," he shouted again. "Jackson will lead you. Follow me!" More men paused; a few turned back toward the enemy. Seeing their reaction, Jackson dropped his reins and grabbed a Confederate battle flag from the hands of its startled bearer. Waving both scabbard and flag above his head, Jackson further emboldened the troops. It was a gesture far surpassing his famous stand at Manassas, where he had earned the sobriquet "Stonewall." Faltering men turned resolute. Exhausted men revived. Scared and panic-stricken men grew ashamed. Lines re-formed; a counterattack began. These soldiers would follow Old Jack "into the jaws of death itself."

The situation was also saved by the arrival of A.P. Hill's Division. Hill, already stripped to his famous red battle shirt and drenched in perspiration, saw what to do next. Unwilling to be outdone by Jackson, Hill waved his unsheathed sword overhead and pushed his relatively fresh troops into action on Stonewall's left.

It was past 6:30 P.M. by then, and the sudden reversal stunned Federal commanders. The order to attack had sent hearts pumping, and the initial successes had been exhilarating. Then came the counterattack by Jackson and Hill, and the wheatfield and cornfield on either side of the Culpeper Road were suddenly littered with dead and wounded men from stout regiments like the 5th Connecticut (92 casualties), 46th Pennsylvania (133 casualties), 28th New York (100 casualties), and 10th Maine (169 casualties) of Crawford's Brigade, and the 3rd Wisconsin (83 casualties) and 2nd Massachusetts

(133 casualties) of General George H. Gordon's Brigade. The Federal toll rose at a horrifying rate. Captain Robert Gould Shaw of the 2nd Massachusetts, who claimed at one point in the fighting the Confederate riflemen were so close that he could "distinguish all their features," estimated that his regiment was "not under fire more than thirty minutes."

The reversal stopped short of being a rout. Blue infantrymen paused, reloaded, and fired as they fell back; they carried

Robert Gould Shaw: Born Massachusetts 1837; from a prominent Boston family, Shaw attended Harvard from 1856 to 1859, but did not graduate; attracted to the mounting sectional crisis, he enlisted as a private in the 7th New York Infantry in April 1861; in May he became a 2d lieutenant in the 2d Massachusetts and made

1st lieutenant in July; promoted to captain in August 1862, Shaw was selected by the governor of Massachusetts to raise a regiment of black troops for service in the Federal army; Shaw approached his new assignment with zeal and in April 1863 was commissioned colonel of the 54th Massachusetts, the first black regiment organized in a free state; the following month the 54th was mustered into Federal service and was sent to South Carolina; in July Shaw led his new command in minor actions on James Island, before moving to Morris Island for operations against Battery Wagner; he requested and received a leading role for his regiment in the planned assault; on 18 July the Federals attacked with Shaw and the 54th in the lead; although courageously mounted, the charge was a disaster that claimed more than a quarter of the regiment, with Colonel Shaw counted among the dead; Confederates, who had long promised bitter reprisals for white officers who commanded black troops, buried Shaw in a common grave with his fallen men; Shaw's parents rejected suggestions to retrieve the colonel's body, believing that their son would have preferred the burial he received; Shaw's regiment, though severely battered, had dispelled many preconceived notions regarding black troops; they could fight and die as bravely as white soldiers.

JACKSON AND POPE AT CEDAR MOUNTAIN 47

wounded comrades to the rear. Yet they were pummeled by the Virginians and North Carolinians in their front and could not withstand the "terrible fire from the bushes and woods." As the 2nd Massachusetts advanced haltingly over "an immense number of bodies" that already littered the wheatfield, they faced a long line of ghost-like Rebel battalions nearly concealed by smoke. The New Englanders' assault seemed to break the Rebel lines, but as the regiment drew nearer, they became trapped in a wicked crossfire. Men were riddled by a "shower of bullets, as if it were so much rain." The regimental flag was shot "through and through, the staff shattered and broken." So were Federal spirits.

Black humor punctuated the Federal reversal. General Alpheus Williams, a Michigan judge, newspaper editor, and politician who commanded the division on the Union right flank, could not help but laugh at "the skedaddle" of Pope, Banks, and their staff officers as the blue tide suddenly cascaded back toward them. Pope, who did not arrive on the battlefield until most of the damage had been done, saw nothing funny in the disaster. He must have cursed the upstart politician Banks for playing the part of Napoleon. And he certainly would have missed the humor in the remark of one retreating soldier who, as he headed for safety, called out to an advancing column of belated reinforcements, "Give 'em hell boys, we got 'em started."

But Banks wanted to try one more attack, a cavalry charge against the Confederate left. Standing in the middle of the cornfield and on a slight rise, Colonel Walker and his 13th Virginia saw the threat. Walker had been cool under pressure all day, and he had directed his sometimes weary men with an enthusiasm that aroused and inspired them. Once more, he prepared to rally the regiment. Waving his hat in one hand and his sword in the other, Walker cried out, "Thirteenth, left wheel!" The men responded instantly, as they did again when Walker sent them at the double toward Culpeper Road. When but ten yards from a rail fence that flanked the road, the regiment halted and delivered a murderous volley into the horribly vulnerable 1st Pennsylvania Cavalry.

The Pennsylvanians, thundering down the road in columns of four, looked magnificent as they charged Taliaferro's division, but courage and discipline were never a match for an ambush. Only at the last minute did they see the Virginians on their flank, too late to escape the slaughter. Lead riders and horses collapsed in a heap. Following ranks piled into one another. Horses wheeled and plunged. Orderly retreat became impossible, and all the while troopers and mounts remained under a heavy cross-fire. A dozen, two dozen, eight dozen Yankees fell. The Pennsylvanians gradually extracted themselves, but they left behind more than half of 164 men. By then it was 7 P.M., and the battle was nearly over.

By 8 P.M., night cradled the battlefield. Jackson ordered A.P. Hill's relatively fresh brigades to pursue the Federals, already pouring back toward Culpeper Court House. Jackson's blood was up. He envisioned pushing Pope across the Rappahannock River before morning, but he was overly optimistic. Sigel had finally arrived, and part of his corps collided with Hill's Division two miles beyond the battlefield. Both sides were startled. Skirmishers rushed forward to exchange fire; gunners wheeled artillery into place and blazed away blindly in the "hottest" exchange of the whole engagement. To the exhausted Confederate infantry, many of whom had by then plopped down to rest, the artillery exchange became a grand fireworks display to cap a triumphant day.

Jackson, deciding it was "imprudent" to press the attack, ordered his command to bivouac for the night. Many Rebels, in sore need of a spot of repose, dropped where they stood. Others, craving water, submerged their faces in one of the two branches of Cedar Run, which ran across the eastern edge of the plain and along the base of the mountain. They either did not notice or did not care that the creek ran red with blood, for dead men and horses littered the banks and lay in the water itself. They ignored the foulness of the water, just as they were oblivious to their clothes, crusted with mud and blood, soaked with sweat, alive with lice and vermin. Having long since learned to live with these conditions, the men were "past caring" about appearance, comfort, and cleanliness. The Rebels had lost over 1,400 killed and wounded of 20,000 men engaged in the fight. The Federals had suffered some 2,600 casualties among their 15,000 combatants.

4

LEE'S COUNTERATTACK

August 10 opened on a ghastly scene. Dead and wounded men and horses, equipment of all varieties littered the battlefield. The early stages of rigor mortis lent the dead a grotesque appearance. Bodies had been "torn and mangled in a dreadful manner." Men disemboweled, men decapitated, limbless men, faceless men, sights and smells people could never imagine in ordinary times. Pope asked Jackson for a truce on August 11 to collect his wounded and bury his dead. Jackson agreed. Yanks and Rebels alike buried their corpses in long trenches or shallow ravines with a thin covering of earth. The stench of the battlefield became overpowering as the temperature rose well past ninety degrees by early afternoon of the eleventh.

Generals James E.B. Stuart, who had arrived with additional cavalry, and Early supervised the truce on behalf of Jackson; Generals Benjamin S. Roberts and George L. Hartsuff represented Pope. As the four generals, accompanied by several other officers, conferred along Cedar Run, their formal and somber introductions soon gave way to jests and reminiscences of earlier days. The whole affair began to look like a "roadside gossip" among farmers. Similarly surreal scenes were played out across the field as Yankees and Rebels conversed matter-of-factly amid the carnage. "The fact that many men get so accustomed to the thing," mused Robert Gould Shaw, "that they can step about among heaps of dead bodies, many of them their best friends and acquaintances, without any particular emotion, is the worst of it all."

But even as the adversaries gossiped and labored in the cornfield, Jackson prepared to withdraw across the Rapidan. Federal reinforcements were already approaching, and he had stung Pope sufficiently to fall back with honor to await Lee. Then, together, they would advance to liberate Culpeper and destroy the miscreant. So back trudged the army. Jackson's men were used to it. "Man that is born of a woman, and enlisteth in Jackson's army, is of few days and short rations," groaned one soldier in a parody of Job that would have shocked the puritanical Jackson.

Horses felled during the Battle of Cedar Mountain, a grim reminder of the devastation of the war.

James Ewell Brown Stuart: born Virginia 1833; of Scotch-Irish and Welsh ancestry, "Jeb" Stuart attended Emory and Henry College 1848–50; graduated thirteenth in the class of 1854 at the U.S. Military Academy; and distinguished himself at West Point by his "almost thankful acceptance" of every offer to fight, although often beaten. Appointed 2d lieutenant in 1st Cavalry and served for six years on the Indian frontier, where he was wounded; promoted to 1st lieutenant in 1855;

married Flora, daughter of Colonel Philip St. George Cooke. In 1859, while on leave, he served as Colonel Robert E. Lee's aide in suppressing John Brown's slave rebellion at Harpers Ferry, Va.; promoted to captain in 1861, less than a month before he resigned from the U.S. Army to join the Confederacy; in 1861 he commanded the 1st Virginia Cavalry at First Manassas and later received promotion to brigadier general; in 1862 he commanded the cavalry during the Peninsula Campaign; executed his first "ride around McClellan," ascertaining the Federal army's exact location; screened the left flank of Lee's army during the Seven Days' Battles. Promoted to major general and given command of Lee's cavalry just prior to the Second Manassas Campaign, Stuart led several raids against Federal forces; participated in the Antietam Campaign, making another spectacular ride around McClellan's army, and commanded his cavalry division at Fredericksburg; in 1863 he temporarily commanded Jackson's Corps at Chancellorsville, after Stonewall and A. P. Hill had been wounded; directed cavalry actions at Brandy Station, the largest and "first true cavalry combat" of the war; conducted a raid during the Gettysburg Campaign for which he received severe criticism; after fighting in the Wilderness and at Spotsylvania, Stuart received a mortal wound at Yellow Tavern on May 11, 1864, and died the next day. He dressed dramatically, with a peacock's plume in his hat and a red flower or a ribbon in his lapel, rode splendid horses, and wore a massive and flowing beard to hide his receding chin, which won him the nickname "Beauty" at West Point. He loved music, dancing, pretty girls, and much jollity, but disallowed drinking or swearing in his presence. Scholars acknowledge Stuart's vanity and exhibitionism along with his bravery, endurance, good humor, and greatness as a cavalryman. Lee, who considered Stuart "the eyes of his army," said of him: "He never brought me a piece of false information."

When Pope learned of the retrograde movement he gloated. Jackson was fleeing for his life "under cover of the night," he reported to Halleck. But the general in chief knew better. "Beware of a snare," he cautioned Pope by telegraph. "Feigned retreats are secesh tactics." Halleck ordered reinforcements from the Army of the Potomac to Culpeper and suggested that "under existing circumstances" Pope should send his locomotives and rolling stock above the Rappahannock on the Orange & Alexandria Railroad and place a strong guard at the bridge. Culpeper County had been selected as the principal point of invasion because the O&A provided Federal forces with a line of communication and supplies from Alexandria through Manassas. Now Pope might need the railroad to evacuate his army. "Do not," Halleck commanded, "advance your force across the Rapidan."

Pope's surgeons continued over the next few days to mend the army. "Culpeper is one vast hospital," asserted a stunned witness. Hospital flags adorned half the homes at the Court House. Local doctors pitched in to assist army physicians, and local families, both Unionist and Rebel, volunteered to help. One Unionist marveled at the way staunch Confederates took Federal wounded into their homes, "notwithstanding the fact that they had been for the previous two weeks most sadly abused" by those same soldiers. Burial teams interred not a few Yankees at a local cemetery. Some dead officers were "packed in charcoal to go to Washington, where they will be put in metallic coffins [and shipped home]," reported Captain Shaw.

On August 13, Clara Barton arrived via railroad with two assistants and piles of medical supplies. This was the first time that Barton had ministered to men in the field. Dr. James Dunn, a Pennsylvania surgeon, welcomed this "homely angel"—Clara was not a beauty—and marveled at her emotional and physical stamina. To attend limbless men, half delirious and wallowing in blood and filth, required "sinews of

Clarissa Harlowe Barton: born Massachusetts 1821; at fifteen began teaching in district schools; later she organized a school for millworkers' children; in 1851 she studied at the Liberal Institute in New York; taught in Bordentown, N.J., where she persuaded the school board to institute free schooling; when opposition to a woman being in charge of such a large school arose and a male principal replaced her, Barton resigned and ended her teaching career; she moved to Washington, D.C., and obtained employment in the Patent Office. In 1861 she began her wartime service by helping supply the needs of the 6th Massachusetts Infantry

Regiment, which had lost much of its baggage after being attacked by civilians while passing through Baltimore; thereafter she advertised for supplies to aid soldiers and received bountiful amounts which she distributed; in 1862 she secured permission to take provisions to the battle-fields and to tend the wounded; thereafter she continued rendering heroic service by getting sup-plies to the front, distributing them, and minister-ing to the wounded; in 1864 she acted as superin-tendent of nurses with the Army of the James, but Barton never had any official connection with the army; although not primarily a hospital nurse, she secured supplies for the relief of suffering, and dis-played courage, endurance, and resourcefulness on the battlefield. After the war she searched for missing soldiers and lectured on her wartime expe-riences; in 1869 she went abroad to recuperate from illness and became involved with the International Red Cross of Geneva, doing relief work under its auspices during the Franco-Prussian War for which she received honors from European royalty; after hard work she finally established the Red Cross in the U.S. in 1881; she spent the latter part of her life directing the organization until she resigned in 1904; she died at Glen Echo near Washington, D.C., in 1912. A slender woman, noted for her grit and determination, who squared her shoulders to any task, Barton spoke with authority and kept abreast of public affairs; her gift was the ability to see what needed to be done and to do it; her independent execution of operations some-times caused controversy, but hard work and dedication earned her the title "angel of the battlefield."

steel and nerves of iron." The little Massachusetts woman possessed both.

With a pause in the fighting, many Union troops also reverted to their habit of living off the civilian population, still justified, as they saw it, by Pope's orders. "Vegetables, fruit, corn and every thing that could be used," recorded one embarrassed soldier, "are swept as clean as if a swarm of Pharo's locusts had been here." It was easy to rob and bully these people, particularly the poorer folk, for the Federals despised them as ignorant barbarians. "They are about the poorest specimens of humanity I have met with," concluded one officer, "having more of the vices of civilization, and less of that native manliness we find even among the wild Bedouins." He pitied this "poor white trash" in some ways, for he believed them to be the "worst victims of slavery, stigmatized by the haughty slaveholders." Yet, ultimately, he held them in "contempt."

Meantime, Pope had decided to abandon Culpeper. Shortly after Pope and Jackson collided at Cedar Mountain, Robert E. Lee became convinced that McClellan would evacuate the Peninsula to reinforce Pope. If McClellan and General Ambrose Burnside, who had, in fact, been sent from the Peninsula to Fredericksburg in early August with the newly constituted Ninth Corps, combined south of the Rappahannock, Lee knew he would have the devil's own time pushing them back across. Burnside had already sent two of his three divisions, led by generals Jesse Reno and Isaac I. Stevens, to join Pope. Thus Lee decided to link forces with Jackson and strike Pope before this potential force could be completely assembled, and before Pope led his so-called Army of Virginia any deeper into the state. Lee moved to Gordonsville on August 13; by August 18, having joined Jackson in Orange County with the five divisions and artillery of General James Longstreet's Corps, he was ready to cross the Rapidan into Culpeper. When Pope learned from pickets, spies, and captured documents (taken from a luckless member of Jeb Stuart's staff) that the game was afoot, he ordered his army to recross the Rappahannock, fortify the northern bank, and dare Lee to attack.

Pope's army, moving lethargically, betrayed the "characteristic and gloomy calm" of demoralized spirits. Once again an Eastern army had penetrated enemy territory only to turn tail and run. Many Federal officers served as poor models during those dark hours. They appeared "a pretty cynical and misanthropic set," claimed a Massachusetts soldier of his regiment's leaders. "They all say they are sick of the war, and they are down on every General here, except perhaps Sigel." Where they were going, what their mission would be, did not concern them: "No one knows, or seems to care much."

A final round of confiscation and marauding punctuated the

Robert E. Lee: born Virginia 1807; son of Ann Hill (Carter) Lee and Henry "Light-Horse Harry" Lee, who died when Robert was eleven; received early education in Alexandria, Virginia, schools; graduated second in his class at U.S. Military Academy in 1829, without receiving a demerit in four years; appointed 2d lieu-

tenant of engineers in 1829, 1st lieutenant in 1836, and captain in 1838; served at Fort Pulaski, Fort Monroe, Fort Hamilton, and superintended engineering project for St. Louis harbor; married Mary Ann Randolph Custis, whose father's estate of "Arlington" on the Virginia shore of the Potomac opposite Washington became Lee's home in 1857 after the death of his father-in-law; in 1846 Lee, then a captain, joined General Winfield Scott's Vera Cruz expedition and invasion of Mexico; Lee's extraordinary industry and capacity won him a brilliant reputation and the lasting confidence and esteem of Scott; wounded in 1847, Lee won three brevet promotions to major, lieutenant colonel, and colonel for gallant and meritorious conduct in the battles of Cerro Gordo, Contreras, Churubusco, and Chapultepec; served as superintendent of the

exodus. Stray or unattended chickens disappeared into haver-sacks. Soldiers butchered sheep, calves, and hogs on the spot. Men broke ranks to roam the countryside a mile from their column. "Only the strictest watch on the part of the company officers can prevent this straggling," insisted one captain. Even if caught, the men had no end of explanations, "and sometimes the excuse is so droll," confessed the captain, "that one is compelled to laugh in spite of himself." Spotting a private with half a sheep tossed over his shoulder, the captain demanded an explanation. The private swore that he killed the sheep "in self-defense" when, incited by his blue uniform, it attacked him.

Lee had a magnificent view of the retreat from atop Clark Mountain, south of the Rapidan. The sight of thousands of wagons and tens of thousands of men escaping vexed him, for

U.S. Military Academy from 1852 to 1855; promoted to lieutenant colonel 2d Cavalry in 1855; commanded Marines sent to Harper's Ferry to capture John Brown after his raid; promoted to colonel 1st Cavalry in 1861; having refused command of Federal armies, his first Confederate command led to failure at Cheat Mountain in western Virginia; after serving along the South Atlantic coast, he returned to Virginia as military advisor to President Jefferson Davis until June 1862 when he replaced the wounded Joseph E. Johnston in command of forces that became known as the Army of Northern Virginia; for nearly three years, Lee's aggressive campaigns and effective defenses frustrated Union efforts to capture the Confederate capital; not until February 1865—two months before his surrender—did he become over-all commander of Confederate forces; after the war, he accepted the presidency of Washington College (later changed to Washington and Lee University) in Lexington, Virginia, where he remained until his death in 1870. Theodore Roosevelt proclaimed Lee "without exception the very greatest of all the great captains." "Lee possessed every virtue of other great commanders without their vices," announced an orator. "He was a foe without hate; a friend without treachery; a victor without oppression, and a victim without murmuring. He was a public officer without vices; a private citizen without reproach; a Christian without hypocrisy and a man without guile." Bold, modest, and heroic, Lee once confessed that if war were less terrible he would become too fond of it. His greatest biographer characterized him as "a simple gentleman."

even at such a distance, he could identify an army in disarray. Jackson passed the time by executing three soldiers found guilty of desertion. He ordered his men to stand in formation and witness the firing squads in action, so as to take this lesson to heart. "Horrible sight," admitted one Confederate, "but rendered necessary for sake of country."

James Longstreet: born South Carolina 1821; graduated U.S. Military Academy fifty-fourth in his class in 1842; appointed a brevet 2d lieutenant in the 4th Infantry the same year; promoted to 2d lieutenant in the 8th Infantry in 1845, and to 1st lieutenant in 1847; won brevet promotions to captain and major for gallant conduct in the battles of Contreras, Churubusco, and Molino del Rey during the Mexican War; served as regimental adjutant from 1847 to 1849; promoted to captain in 1852 and to major

(paymaster department) in 1858; appointed Confederate brigadier general, served at First Manassas, and promoted to major general in 1861; distinguished service during Peninsular Campaign, Second Manassas, Sharpsburg, and Fredericksburg in 1862; promoted to lieutenant general in 1862, "Old Pete" became General Lee's senior corps commander; on detached service south of the James River in May 1863 thus missing the action at Chancellorsville; commanded right wing of Lee's army at Gettysburg in July 1863; took his corps by rail to Chickamauga, Georgia, in September 1863 to help defeat General William S. Rosecrans, but failed in his attempt to capture Knoxville, Tennessee; returned to Virginia in 1864 in time to participate in the Battle of the Wilderness, where he sustained a critical wound that incapacitated him until late fall; led his corps during closing months of the war in defense of Richmond; surrendered with Lee to Grant at Appomattox Court House; after the war, he settled in New Orleans, became a Republican, and as a state militia officer led black troops against Confederate veterans during Reconstruction disturbances; enjoyed political patronage from Republicans; wrote his war memoirs, *From Manassas to Appomattox*; died at Gainesville, Georgia, in 1904. Lee called Longstreet "my old War Horse." An able battlefield tactician, he was at times stubborn, quarrelsome, and overconfident in his ability as an independent commander.

So Pope's spies and the captured dispatches gave him the jump on Lee, and, to complicate matters, Lee had trouble getting his men across the Rapidan. Confederate troops and supply trains arrived late at the river crossings. Even Lee's cavalry had been delayed. His army, 50,000 strong, finally rumbled forward on August 20. The cavalry bounded ahead to nip at the heels of Pope's rear guard. Lee divided his infantry, consisting of seven divisions and two unattached brigades, into two wings. James Longstreet, commanding the right wing, crossed at Raccoon Ford; Jackson led the left wing across Somerville Ford. The Rebels exuded confidence. They joked and laughed "like a lot of school boys" as they waded across the Rapidan. Many of Longstreet's men, freshly arrived from the Peninsula, seemed anxious to use their new Enfield rifles, "trophies of war" captured from McClellan during the Seven Days.

A series of sharp cavalry skirmishes lent excitement to the chase. A portion of General Fitzhugh Lee's brigade drove frantic Federal pickets across the Rappahannock at Kelly's Ford. General Beverly Robertson's Brigade collided with Federal horsemen between Stevensburg and Brandy Station. The Rebels charged "with loud shouts and wild yelling" to catch Colonel Judson Kilpatrick's 2d New York Cavalry in the rear. Colonel Joseph Karge's 1st New Jersey launched an ill-coordinated countercharge, but after some early promise of success, Karge was wounded and his regiment broken. General George D. Bayard saved the situation by dismounting his men and forming a skirmish line in a patch of woods. Their concentrated carbine fire halted further pursuit and bought enough time for a safe river crossing.

Culpeper's citizens poured out to greet Lee's advancing columns. "God preserve you, my boys!" shouted a grateful gentleman as each regiment passed his gate. Women dispensed water to parched throats along the roadside. Joseph Gorrell, a druggist at Culpeper Court House, hauled out a large tub of lemonade to distribute along Main Street. "Just think of it!"

exclaimed one of his beneficiaries. "Ice cold lemonade, with plenty of lemon in it to make it sour, and plenty of sugar to make it sweet, and ice to make it cold, to a tired, weary, dirty, dusty Confederate soldier, on a hot day in August." Gorrell could not match the ladies in other ways. Young women rushed forward waving handkerchiefs and flirting violently with the gallant knights and men-at-arms. Some of them positively swooned at the sight of the most handsome and famous warriors, like Jeb Stuart. Older women contented themselves with kissing passing battle flags and shedding tears of joy. Men, women, and children, "many thanking God on their knees for their deliverance from the enemy," surged around their liberators.

Soldiers and accompanying journalists soon understood why the people rejoiced. "The people all have the same tales to tell," reported a member of the Richmond Howitzers. "They [the Yankees] took everything they could lay their hands on & not content with that would break up costly furniture, tear down banisters, kick the panels out of doors, etc." A newspaper correspondent expressed shock at the "melancholy picture of desolation and devastation." The "unbridled license" of Pope's soldiers, he learned, had left the county "almost a desert." "Unoffending citizens have been impoverished in a day," he reported, "their fencing destroyed, their sheep and hogs and cattle butchered, their grain entirely consumed, their horses all stolen....Many a family has been left in a condition verging upon absolute want and starvation." One officer had seen nothing like it in over a year of war. The "scene of confusion" he witnessed at one farm, with "pieces of broken chairs & furniture scattered in all directions, broken panes of glass, feathers," stunned him. Outside, the fences had nearly disappeared, and not so much as a potato remained in the garden.

By nightfall, the rest of Lee's army had arrived in Culpeper. Longstreet's infantry, which had trudged across the southeastern corner of the county, drew up at Kelly's Ford, directly opposite Pope's left flank. Jackson's men followed on Longstreet's left and halted near Stevensburg. Stuart's cavalry fell back around Brandy Station. Lee also bivouacked near Brandy. Despite their cheerfulness, Lee's men sighed gratefully for the night. The march had been long, hot, and dusty. The sun blistered their skin, their wool uniforms chafed, and ill-fitting shoes pinched and rubbed at every step. "O, my country, how I bleed for thee!" sang one wag as the columns snaked through the countryside. The rest of his regiment picked up the lament, though "never in a seditious or complaining way," stressed a Virginian, "for a truer or more loyal set of men never marched beneath a banner."

But a bivouac meant water, food, sleep. Their arms stacked, the men prepared a supper of green corn. Their corn eaten, tired men threw themselves on the ground. They felt the weariness and fatigue ebb from their bodies, absorbed by the sweet grass and benevolent earth. They slept without tents, though each man rolled himself in a blanket. The night turned chilly and damp, and nights on campaign, they knew from experience, were always brief. The men treasured every hour of sleep as one in which they might be "lost to the world and its cares, dreaming of home." Their campfires, twinkling in the cool, fresh air, offered a picturesque sight. As Lee gazed into the night, he felt satisfied. Pope, safely at bay across the river, posed no threat.

The next morning, August 21, after breakfasting on rye coffee, bread, and honey, Lee ordered Jackson's wing to join Longstreet along the Rappahannock. Stuart's men were already probing, challenging, looking for a way to get at Pope. Some cavalry regiments actually crossed the river in anticipation of an immediate attack, but Lee recalled them. He intended to anchor his right flank between Kelly's Ford and the Rappahannock bridge with Longstreet's wing, then cautiously push his remaining forces up the river as far as Jeffersonton. This would stretch his line dangerously thin, but he knew Pope would feel obliged to do the same.

Lee remained anxious. He now understood that Pope's position was too strong to risk a direct assault across the river. He would have to gain Pope's flank or rear by means of some "practicable fords" in order to shift the war away from Richmond and the James River. Yet outwardly Marse Robert remained unflappable. An admiring private in the 21st Virginia Infantry puzzled over Lee's apparent timidness in plunging after Pope, but Uncle Bob retained the man's confidence. "I have seen him several times today," he excitedly informed his parents, "& as he looks easy and cheerful I dare say he knows what he is about & will let the Yankees know when the proper time arrives."

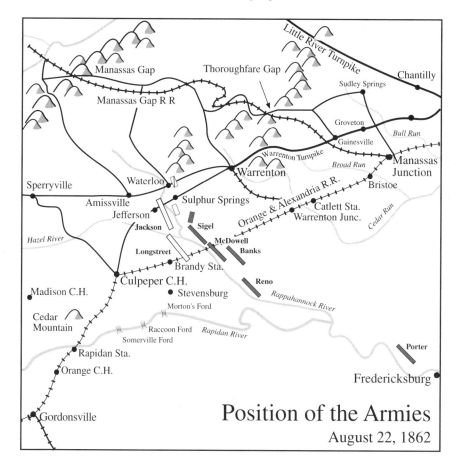

Position of the Armies
August 22, 1862

Lee made his initial move on August 22. Fifteen hundred of Stuart's cavalry dashed across Waterloo Bridge and the ford at Hart's Mill that morning. Their objective was Catlett's Station, fourteen miles to the east on the Orange & Alexandria Railroad, where Stuart planned to destroy the bridge across Cedar Creek and sever Pope's communications. The cavalrymen thundered through token resistance at the station to capture over 300 men, a Yankee payroll worth $500,000 in greenbacks and $20,000 in gold, huge amounts of personal equipment and baggage, tons of supplies, and untold horses, mules, and wagons. They found so much booty that Stuart had to destroy most of it. He nearly captured a train, too, which had just departed Catlett's for Alexandria.

By then, torrential rain battered the column. Stuart's men cut the telegraph wires, but the rain and a company of Federal skirmishers on the opposite bank kept them from destroying the railroad bridge. Still, Stuart returned satisfied to Culpeper. It was his finest hour since the ride around McClellan's army on the Peninsula, and he was especially pleased with one bit of boodle: Pope's personal baggage, including his uniforms and dispatch book. The book included not only Pope's correspondence with Halleck but also the deployment of his army.

By August 25, the skies had cleared enough for Lee to attempt another crossing. With Stuart's cavalry preceding him, and Longstreet creating a diversion between Sulphur Springs and Waterloo, Jackson pushed his infantry across the Rappahannock at Hinson's Mill, four miles above Waterloo. Lee wanted Jackson to gain Pope's rear by marching around his right flank. If Stonewall could seize Pope's supply depot at Manassas Junction and cut the telegraph lines between that point and Alexandria, Pope would be forced to fall back. Then Lee could cross the river unopposed and crush the "miscreant" between the two wings of his army.

Jackson maneuvered to perfection. Gaining Pope's flank, he cut behind him through Thoroughfare Gap to destroy a Federal supply train at Bristoe Station before turning his corps north to secure Manassas. Pope, hopeful that aggressive action might yet save the situation, pulled back his army on August 27. He intended to pursue, corner, and destroy Jackson before Lee and Longstreet could slip across the Rappahannock. It was a tall order.

5
MANASSAS, AGAIN

Few Confederate soldiers ever enjoyed themselves so thoroughly as did Jackson's men at Manassas Junction on August 27. Hundreds of tons of supplies, even more than the stores taken in Stuart's raid at Catlett's Station, fell to Jackson. "It was hard to decide what to take," recalled a Virginia soldier, so extensive were the treasures to be found. Soldiers rifled warehouses, railroad cars, and sheds in search of food, clothing, shoes, tobacco, whatever struck their fancy. The foodstuffs, especially, excited them. Hungry men luxuriated in bacon, hams, flour, cakes, fruit, coffee, sugar, molasses, mustard, canned oysters, all of it the very stuff of soldiers' dreams.

Jackson did little to curb the riot. God knew his men had earned the prize, if for no other reason than by virtue of having marched fifty-four miles in thirty-six hours. They had accomplished what Jackson knew they could do, and what Lee prayed they might do, gained Pope's rear. They were entitled to their spoils, like buccaneers who had captured a treasure ship. The army could not possibly gather or transport such immense stores, and even to destroy the depot would require much labor and time, more time than Pope would likely grant them. Still, Old Jack did strike one item from the sanctioned list of contraband, and that was liquor. "I fear that liquor more than General Pope's army," he grumbled of the barrels of whiskey and brandy discovered by his troops. Much to the dismay of his men, Stonewall ordered it all spilled onto the ground. "Don't spare a drop, nor let any man taste it under any circumstances," announced the teetotaler.

The men soon had their revelry disrupted in any case. Several rambunctious Union regiments had advanced on Manassas from the east early in the day. These Yankees were easily convinced to retreat. More ominously, Joseph Hooker's Division, one of several that had been detached from the Army of the Potomac to reinforce Pope a few days earlier, was drawing near. But as Hooker turned to strike at the northern half of Lee's divided army, Richard Ewell's Division blocked his path and inflicted 300 casualties in several hours of fighting along Kettle Run, just south of Bristoe Station. The forces disengaged shortly before sunset. Jackson still held the junction, but he knew he must withdraw.

It was a shame, really, for Jackson remained confident that Lee, accompanied by Longstreet's Corps, would join him before Pope posed a serious threat. Yet caution was required, and Jackson also felt certain that McClellan was headed for Manassas. If Little Mac should arrive before Lee, the odds would be terribly lopsided against his gray-clad warriors. So Jackson destroyed the remaining supplies at Manassas and fell back to take a defensive position on a ridge five miles to the north. He placed part of his men in an unfinished railroad cut at the top of the ridge while the rest bedded down on its gentle slope. The withdrawal, otherwise conducted in darkness, was eerily illuminated by a raging fire that consumed hundreds of railroad cars and wagons at the junction—"the grandest con-flagration I ever witnessed," decided one veteran.

And what of McClellan? He never arrived, nor did the fresh corps—some 25,000 additional men—Pope hoped and Halleck expected he would send. Indeed, Halleck would later recall that he had insisted that McClellan dispatch a corps from Alexandria. McClellan claimed the defense of Washington came first. "Pope is in a bad way," he admitted to his wife on August 28, "& I have not yet the force at hand to relieve him." He informed Halleck on that same day that with Jackson at Manassas it was too late to save Pope, and that "it would be a sacrifice to send them [reinforcements] out now." Of course, McClellan despised Pope as an upstart who not only defied all gentlemanly rules of war but who also coveted his job. He would shed no tears if Pope were annihilated. Pope's best bet, McClellan told Halleck, was to fight his way back to the capital.

Annihilation and retreat were the furthest things from Pope's mind. He smelled victory. With an incredible lack of appreciation for his precarious strategic situation, Pope decid-ed on the evening of August 27 that he had trapped Jackson. All he need do was advance and launch an assault the follow-ing morning. Hooker's Division had been sent to locate Jackson's command. The remainder of Pope's army would pur-sue, corner, and defeat Stonewall. "I believed then," Pope later claimed, "that we were sufficiently in advance of Longstreet...that by using our whole force vigorously we should be able to crush Jackson completely before Longstreet could have reached the scene of action."

However, Pope had assumed he would find Jackson at Manassas, and that his subordinates would display some ini-tiative. Neither happened. Jackson had slipped Pope's noose, and several of Pope's commanders moved too slowly to bag their prey. Not that Jackson's own movements had been flaw-less. Stonewall's secretive nature emerged yet again, and his vague orders to Ewell left several of his divisions marching in circles before they finally stumbled into Jackson's chosen line of defense on the evening of the twenty-seventh. When the head of Pope's column, now led by General Philip Kearny's

Philip Kearny: born New York 1815; from an extremely wealthy family, Kearny was graduated from Columbia University in 1833 and studied law; although he desired a military career, his family discouraged him; he travelled extensively and in 1836 became a millionaire on the death of his grandfather, but he never abandoned his martial aspirations; he was granted a 2d lieutenant's commission in his uncle Stephen Watts Kearny's 1st Dragoons; after attending cavalry school in

France in 1839, he served in the Chasseurs d' Afrique in Algeria; he returned to the U.S. in the early 1840s and served as aide-de-camp to Generals in Chief Alexander Macomb and Winfield Scott; promoted to 1st lieutenant and then to captain, Kearny was brevetted to major for gallantry in the Battle of Churubusco, in which he lost his left arm; he resigned his captain's commission in 1851 and retired to his New Jersey estate; returning to Europe in the late 1850s, he served in the French cavalry during the War for Italian Independence and distinguished himself at Magenta and Solferino, winning the Legion of Honor; returning to the U.S. with the onset of the Civil War, Kearny became in August 1861 one of the first to receive a brigadier general's commission in the U.S. Volunteers; he commanded a brigade in the Army of the Potomac during General George B. McClellan's spring 1862 Peninsula Campaign and led a division with marked skill during the Seven Days' Battles; promoted to major general of volunteers in July, he developed the "Kearny Patch" to identify the men of his division, which became the prototype for the Federal corps badge system; sent with his division to join General John Pope's Army of Virginia, he served credibly during the Second Bull Run Campaign; on 1 September 1862, during the rear-guard action at Chantilly, Kearny accidently rode into the Confederate lines and was killed; his remains were returned to the Federal lines under a flag of truce. A splendid horseman with a powerful battlefield presence, Kearny was highly regarded by his soldiers and fellow officers; his loss was a serious blow to the Army of the Potomac.

Division from the Army of the Potomac, reached the junction around noon the following day, it found not the Rebels but the smoldering remains and scattered remnants of a once magnifi-

Rufus King: born New York 1814; King was graduated from the U.S. Military Academy in 1833, fourth in his class of forty-three; commissioned a brevet 2d lieutenant of engineers, he served only three years before resigning to become a civil engineer; during the prewar years he had a varied career as a newspaper editor in New York and Wisconsin, adjutant general of New York, and advocate of public education in Wisconsin; although appointed minister to the Vatican by President Abraham Lincoln, King never assumed the position, instead resigning to raise a Wisconsin brigade for Federal service; among the first to be commissioned a brigadier general in the volunteer army, he organized the unit that became the famed "Iron Brigade"; he commanded the brigade and then a division in northern Virginia, before joining General John Pope's Army of Virginia in June 1862; during the Second Bull Run Campaign, King's premature withdrawal, without orders, from Gainesville compelled General James Ricketts to abandon Thoroughfare Gap, thus allowing the Confederate army to concentrate at Manassas; although King's division performed admirably against "Stonewall" Jackson's Corps at Groveton, King himself was said to have been drunk; a court of inquiry convened following the Federal debacle at Bull Run

found that King had disobeyed orders and erred in judgement in withdrawing from Gainesville; removed from his division, he was given a minor command in southeast Virginia; in a ridiculous example of official impropriety, King was appointed to the court-martial that convicted Fitz John Porter, whom Pope had blamed for the disaster at Second Bull Run; after heading a division in the Washington defenses, King, an epileptic, resigned from the army for reasons of health; thereafter, he reclaimed his assignment as minister to the Vatican; in Italy, he assisted in the apprehension of Lincoln assassination conspirator John Surratt, who had fled to Europe to avoid capture; returning to the United States in 1868, King was a customs agent at New York City; he died there in 1876.

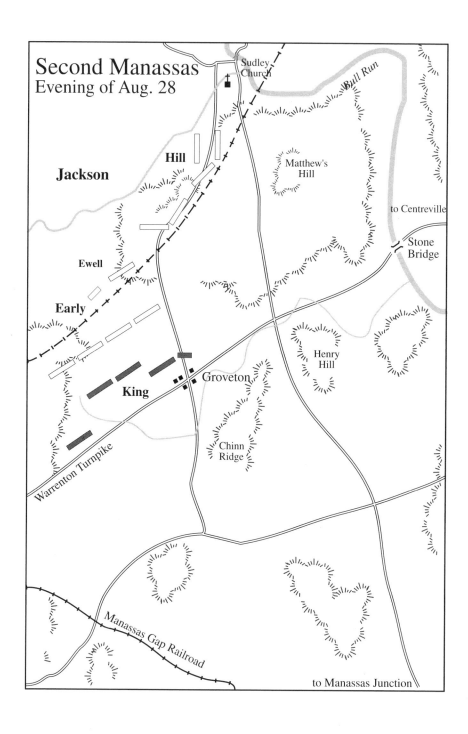

Second Manassas
Evening of Aug. 28

cent supply depot. "The whole plain as far as the eye could reach," reported a Yankee officer, "was covered with boxes, barrels, military equipment, cooking utensils, bread, meat, and beans lying in the wildest confusion."

Pope, learning that Jackson had escaped, assumed that he had retreated to Centreville, an impression reinforced by erroneous reports from captured Rebel stragglers. Corps commander Irvin McDowell, responding to Pope's excitement, ordered General Rufus King's Division to pursue Stonewall. Thus began three days of some of the most intense fighting of the war.

At about 6:00 P.M., King's four brigades ambled along the Warrenton Turnpike directly toward Jackson's lines. Old Jack could not believe his luck. He had been agitated all day, impatient for Longstreet to arrive, hesitant to unleash his own force against an army twice his size, and all the while fearing that Pope would escape. Now, miraculously, Pope had come to him. It seemed too good to be true; any moment he expected the blue column to halt or turn back. When at last it became clear that King meant to pass right before his guns, no more than a few hundred yards away, Jackson could not contain himself. "Bring out your men, gentlemen," he ordered his staff.

The first Rebel rounds fell short of the target, a portent of things to come. Jackson had strung his force too far—nearly two miles—to concentrate effectively. The Federals, for their part, maneuvered quickly from columns into lines, but they had advanced too late in the day to put a dent in Jackson's right flank. Bluecoats and graycoats raked one another with horrendous sheets of musket and rifle fire along a thousand-yard front. Well-dressed lines became ragged crowds, reported a Wisconsin officer, as the two sides pushed to within fifty yards, all the while "pouring musketry into each other as rapidly as men could load and shoot."

The Confederates, who did most of the attacking, suffered for their boldness. "No rebel of that column who escaped death," swore a New Yorker about one attack, "will ever forget that volley. It seemed like one gun." General Isaac R. Trimble, commanding a brigade in Ewell's Corps, agreed: "I have never known so terrible a fire as raged for over an hour on both

Isaac R. Trimble: born Virginia 1802; raised in Kentucky, Trimble was graduated from the U.S. Military Academy in 1822, seventeenth in his class of forty; after ten years' service in the artillery, he resigned his lieutenant's commission to enter the fledgling railroad industry; he settled in Maryland and spent the next three decades

in railroad engineering; when the secession crises came to a head, Trimble assisted in the sabotage of several bridges leading to the Federal capital; since Maryland did not secede, he offered his services to his state of birth; commissioned a colonel of engineers in Virginia's state forces in May 1861, he was appointed brigadier general in Confederate service in August; given command of an infantry brigade in early 1862, Trimble distinguished himself during General T.J. "Stonewall" Jackson's Shenandoah Valley Campaign, most notably in the action at Cross Keys; he took part in the Seven Days' Battles and played a conspicuous role at Cedar Mountain and Manassas Junction in August 1862; severely wounded in the leg at Second Manassas, he was disabled for most of a year; his performance, though, did not go unnoticed; he received promotion to major general to rank from January 1863; after commanding the (Shenandoah) Valley District in June, Trimble, without an assigned command, accompanied the Army of Northern Virginia on the invasion of Pennsylvania; during the Battle of Gettysburg in July 1863, he assumed command of the wounded General Dorsey Pender's Division and led it during Pickett's Charge; again severely wounded in the leg, he was unable to join the army's retreat and became a prisoner of the victorious Federals; after the amputation of his damaged limb, Trimble remained imprisoned until exchanged in March 1865; en route to rejoin the army, he learned of General Robert E. Lee's surrender at Appomattox; after the war he resided in Baltimore, where he died in 1888. Although General Trimble was among the oldest officers to hold a field command, he was a vigorous campaigner, well respected by his soldiers and superiors alike; his wounds no doubt precluded a larger role in the conflict.

sides. The dead and wounded bore next morning melancholy evidence of its severity." Brave men withstood the onslaughts for over two hours, until darkness forced a cease fire. By then, the 21st and 26th Georgia regiments had together lost 70 percent of their men. The Stonewall Brigade had lost 340 of 800 men. Generals fell, too. Richard Ewell had his left leg shattered by a Yankee bullet. He would be a one-legged man by the next morning.

Roughly one-third of the men engaged on both sides had been killed or wounded, and as the Yankees fell back, their field hospitals—to be found in houses, sheds, and tents across the countryside—could not possibly hold all who required attention. It was far worse than Cedar Mountain. The 2d Wisconsin, which had blunted the earliest Confederate charge, lost 276 of 430 engaged, and twenty-one of their wounded had been shot at least twice. The 19th Indiana lost 210 men; the 76th New York and 56th Pennsylvania together lost 236 men. Many soldiers wondered how anyone could have escaped the rain of shot and shell. Yet, terrible as the firing had been, the most vivid memory for many bluecoats, especially new recruits, proved to be the unnerving Rebel yell. "That yell," insisted a Wisconsin Badger, "there is nothing like it this side of the infernal region, and the peculiar corkscrew sensation that it sends down your backbone under the circumstances can never be told."

Jackson muttered about missed opportunities. He had outnumbered King three to one and enjoyed the element of surprise, but his inability to launch a coordinated assault against the admittedly stout defense of the surprised Federals soured the day. He might have inflicted heavy casualties, but the Yankees, in return, had gained knowledge of his position. No longer confident that Longstreet would arrive in time to reinforce him, Jackson positioned his entire command behind the natural earthwork of the railroad cut and braced himself for the next morning's inevitable Federal attack.

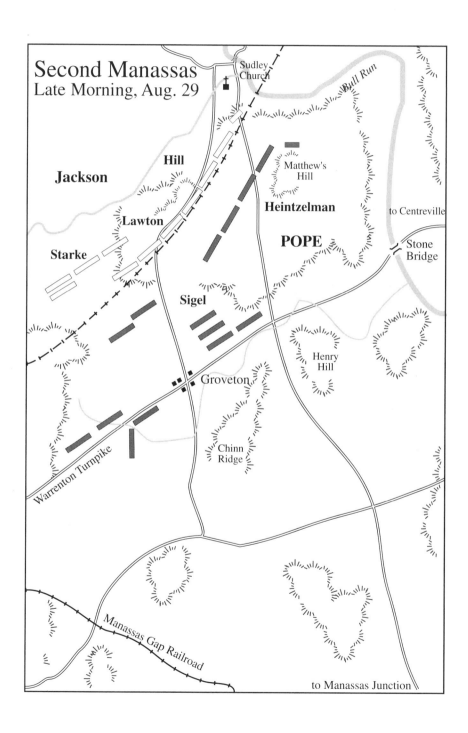

Second Manassas
Late Morning, Aug. 29

Sudley
Church

Bull Run

to Centreville

Stone
Bridge

Jackson

Hill

Matthew's
Hill

Heintzelman

Lawton

POPE

Starke

Sigel

Henry
Hill

Groveton

Chinn
Ridge

Warrenton Turnpike

Manassas Gap Railroad

to Manassas Junction

Jackson need not have worried, for Pope persisted in a dangerous frame of mind: he remained overconfident. From the day he assumed command of the army, despite setbacks in Culpeper, on the Rappahannock, at Catlett's Station, and along the Warrenton Turnpike, Pope had never doubted his ability to thrash the Rebels. While chuckling at his bluster, the army had at first believed in him. Fewer men retained their faith on the evening of August 28. Pope's officers expressed bewilderment over their commander's failure to understand how close King's division had come to disaster. When Pope ordered Phil Kearny to move forward shortly after midnight, in preparation for a dawn attack, Kearny exploded, "Tell General Pope to go to Hell." His men needed rest and nourishment, insisted Kearny: "We won't march before morning."

Pope intended to make a swift converging attack against Jackson on August 29. The initial Federal advance, again aimed at the right center of his line, began at daybreak. Franz Sigel's men did the dirty work, with one exuberant brigade commander shouting, "Fall in boys; we're going to whip them before breakfast." Stonewall feared they might. He knew himself to be outnumbered, and if Sigel's assault were to be followed by similar pressure against his entire front, the day would end badly for him. Lee and Longstreet must come soon, grumbled Jackson. Meantime, Stonewall rode along his line, exhorting the men to bear up: "Two hours, men, only two hours; in two hours you will have help. You must stand it two hours."

The Rebels were saved by Pope's inability to coordinate the movements of his army. By early afternoon, no other Federal corps had entered the fray, and Sigel, seeing his job as one of checking the Confederates until the rest of the army became engaged, failed to push his men. Lee and Longstreet, who had followed Jackson's route to Manassas rather than risk being delayed by Pope's rear guard in a direct pursuit from Culpeper, had broken through light resistance at Thoroughfare Gap and joined a relieved Jackson at midmorning. Fully deployed by 1 P.M., the newcomers extended Stonewall's right flank by another mile. As it turned out, these reinforcements would not lend their weight to the fighting for another twenty-four hours, but just here, on Longstreet's front, unfolded the most bizarre, not to say critical, event of the day.

6
END OF THE MISCREANT

General Fitz John Porter, whose men, like those of
McDowell and Kearny, had been transferred to Pope from the
Army of the Potomac, found himself commanding the extreme
left Union corps on August 29. He had marched his men up
from Bristoe before daylight, and only arrived on the battlefield
at midmorning. A skilled tactician who had led a corps bril-
liantly during the Seven Days, Porter had fallen into an
admirable position from which to smash Jackson's right, fixed,
as it was, by Sigel's attack. Unfortunately, Pope had issued
ambiguous orders to Porter. He had told him to advance and
be poised to attack, but he had not told him to strike. Indeed,
he had hinted that it might be necessary for Porter to fall back
should changing circumstances dictate as much. Yet Pope did
expect Porter to attack, and continued in that expectation for
the remainder of the day. He finally issued a direct order to
advance, but by then, it was nearly nightfall. Pope would have

Porter court martialed that autumn for disloyalty and disobeying orders, and enjoy the perverse satisfaction of seeing Porter dismissed from the service.

Pope always maintained—and some historians have agreed—that he was done in at Second Manassas by the disloyalty not only of Porter but of several other officers from the Army of the Potomac. Porter, in turn, would be convicted at his court martial by a cohort of anti-McClellan officers. He became Pope's scapegoat in a game of army politics, doomed by the fact that he was a disciple of George McClellan. Pope did not trust Porter, and Porter loathed Pope. That was the crux of the matter. Yet the fact remains that Pope's own unre-

Fitz John Porter: born New Hampshire 1822; Porter was graduated from the U.S. Military Academy in 1845, eighth in his class of forty-one; commissioned a 2d lieutenant in the artillery, he severed in the Mexican War, during which he was promoted to 1st lieutenant, wounded at Chapultepec, and earned two brevets for gallantry; thereafter he was an artillery instructor at West Point and served as adjutant to Albert Sidney Johnston during the Utah Expedition; at the outbreak of the Civil

War, Porter was promoted directly from lieutenant to colonel to command the 15th U.S. Infantry; after serving as chief of staff to General Robert Patterson in the Shenandoah Valley, Porter was commissioned into the volunteer army as brigadier general in August 1861; he aided general George B. McClellan, with whom he developed a strong relationship, in the development of the Army of the Potomac; he then commanded a division during McClellan's spring 1862 Peninsula Campaign; commanding the provisional Fifth Corps during the Seven Days' Battles, Porter displayed superb defensive generalship at Mechanicsville, Gaines' Mill, and Malvern Hill; for his actions during the Seven Days, Porter was promoted to major general of volunteers and brevetted brigadier general in the regular army; sent to bolster General John Pope's Army of Virginia during the Second Bull Run

alistic view of the tactical situation on August 29, and his vague orders, account for Porter's inactivity.

Ironically—and here is yet another measure of Pope's misunderstanding of the tactical situation—whatever intrigue may have prevailed within the Union army, Porter's failure to move on August 29 may have saved Pope. Porter's position on the Confederate flank, which actually extended beyond Longstreet's right, prohibited Lee from throwing this wing into the general engagement that day. Had he done so, Pope's command would have been hit hard on the flank and in the rear, crushed perhaps to extinction. As it was, the remainder of the day dissolved into meaningless yet savage attacks and counterattacks along

Campaign, Porter, ever loyal to the temporarily discredited McClellan, openly criticized Pope, whom he despised; during the August 1862 battle of Second Bull Run, Porter refused to execute Pope's misinformed order to attack, an order Porter believed impossible to execute; the battle, a crushing defeat for the Federals, ended Pope's role in the war but destroyed Porter's career; Pope, who was relieved of command, accused Porter of disobedience, disloyalty, and misconduct in the face of the enemy; Porter remained on duty and served under McClellan at Antietam, where his corps was held in reserve; in November 1862 the government acted on Pope's charges and placed Porter under arrest; the subsequent court-marshall, which became as much an attempt to discredit McClellan as to convict Porter, returned a guilty verdict and in January 1863 Porter was dismissed from the army; thereafter, he pursued various business interests, served as New York City's commissioner of police, of the fire department, and of public works; he also declined a position in the Egyptian army; his chief concern, to which he devoted much of his energy, was to clear his name; in 1878 an examining board headed by General John M. Schofield exonerated Porter of all charges connected to his performance at Second Bull Run and further held that his actions had likely prevented an even worse outcome; four years later President Chester Arthur remitted Porter's sentence, but it took another four years for Congress to pass a bill that restored him to the army's roll; on 5 August 1886 he was recommissioned a colonel of infantry to date from May 1861, but was denied back pay; two days later he was retired at his own request; General Porter died at Morristown, New Jersey, in 1901. The Porter case became one of the most unfortunate controversies of the war; one that deprived the Federal army of a most capable officer.

Jackson's front. Pope's frantic attempts to engage his entire army failed, even though, by 5 P.M., he had drawn Jackson's whole corps into the contest. The imbalance was startling, as three Confederate divisions held off ten Federal divisions.

Casualties mounted swiftly, just as they had on the previous evening, from primitive grappling, blind flailing, and point-blank volleys. Jackson could no longer use the hope of being reinforced to spur his men to battle; the reinforcements had arrived. Instead, Old Jack calmly insisted on success. When A. P. Hill, his old nemesis, warned Jackson that his division's dangerously thin ranks (Hill had already lost 500 men) threatened to break, Stonewall replied, "I'll expect you to beat them." In fact, the Yankees did drive Hill back and opened a 300-yard breach in his line, but with the help of reinforcments from Jubal Early's Brigade, Hill closed the gap in a fierce hour of fighting. He relayed word of his success to Jackson via a staff officer. "General Hill presents his compliments," reported the subordinate, "and says the attack of the enemy was repulsed." Jackson indulged in one of his rare smiles and replied, "Tell him I knew he would do it."

It had been a closerun thing for the Rebels, and a "fearfully long" day for all. "Time and again the heavy line of the enemy rolled against us," recalled one of Jackson's staff officers. "Each attack was weaker, each repulse more difficult—the Federals dispirited, the Confederates worn out." Darkness once more produced a nightmarish fugue of cries for water and assistance. Surgeons, who had been engaged since early morning, continued to work through the night, well knowing that, despite their labors, many men who might otherwise have been saved would perish for want of attention.

By the morning of August 30, still more of Pope's officers doubted his ability to lead the army. They knew they should have whipped Jackson on the preceding day. They also knew that Jackson had no thought of retiring; and yet here was Pope, not only still insisting that the Rebels were in flight, but apparently now uncertain of how to catch them. More than that, he seemed not to appreciate that Longstreet had arrived in strength on his left. "General Pope seemed wholly at a loss what to do and what to think," marveled one officer. Pope pondered the situation all morning. By noon, he had devised a plan of pursuit. At 1 P.M., he received word that Longstreet was advancing and threatening to turn his flank. Doubting the report, Pope continued with his original plan, even going so far as to pull Porter's Corps off the left flank and throw it into his fresh advance .

The Army of Virginia lurched into action at 3 P.M. against Jackson's right flank, in a repetition of the previous two days. Some 5,000 Federal troops slammed into Rebel ranks, which quivered but remained secure behind their works. "The yells from both sides were indescribably savage," recognized a New York infantryman. "We were transformed...from a lot of good-natured boys to the most bloodthirsty of demoniacs." A few Federal regiments reached the Confederate slope, some to within a dozen yards of the gray defensive line, but they could not break through. Federals fell in heaps, exposed as they were to a withering fire, while many Confederates benefited from the best natural earthworks they would enjoy during the war. "Regiments got mixed up—brigades were intermingled—all was one seething, anxious, excited mass," recalled a Pennsylvanian. "Men were falling by scores around us, and still we could see no enemy."

In repulsing the Federals on the previous day, some Confederate regiments had nearly run of out of ammunition. On this day, they did so entirely. In their desperation to beat back the relentless Federal pressure, some Rebels, most notably the Louisiana brigade of General William E. Starke, resorted to throwing rocks. "Huge stones began to fall about us," confirmed one attacker, "and now and then one of them would happen to strike one or another of us with very unpleasant effect."

John Bell Hood: born Kentucky 1831; Hood was graduated from the U.S. Military Academy in 1853, forty-fourth in his class of fifty-two that included Philip Sheridan, James B. McPherson, and John M. Schofield; commissioned 2d lieutenant, he served on the frontier most notably with the elite 2d Cavalry, a regiment that included Robert E. Lee, Albert Sidney Johnston, William J. Hardee, George H. Thomas, and many other future Civil War generals; while on duty in Texas, Hood was wounded in an engagement with Comanches; he resigned his 1st lieutenant's commission in 1861 to enter Confederate service at the same grade; he rose quickly through the ranks to major, commanding all cavalry at Yorktown; in October 1861 Hood became colonel of the 4th Texas Infantry; promoted to brigadier general in March 1862, he commanded the Texas Brigade during the Peninsular Campaign and the Seven Days Battles, during which the brigade spearheaded the Confederate breakthrough

at Gaines' Mill; Hood commanded a division at Second Manassas, again delivering a crushing attack, and at Sharpsburg (Antietam), where his division was sacrificed to buy time for Lee's army; promoted to major general, he led his division at Fredericksburg and at Gettysburg, where a wound rendered his left arm virtually useless; returning to duty, he commanded General James Longstreet's Corps in the Confederate breakthrough at Chickamauga but was again wounded, losing his right leg; promoted to lieutenant general in February 1864 (to rank from September 1863), he joined the Army of Tennessee in March; he directed a corps during the Atlanta Campaign until selected to replace General Joseph E. Johnston with the temporary rank of full general; he fought a series of battles around Atlanta but was forced to evacuate that city on September 1, 1864; leading his army into Tennessee, he fought a bloody battle at Franklin in November and was routed at Nashville the following month; relieved at his own request in January 1865, he surrendered at Natchez, Mississippi, in May; after the war he engaged in business in New Orleans, married, and fathered eleven children; General Hood died at New Orleans along with his wife and eldest daughter during the yellow fever epidemic in 1879. As a combat commander, Hood was unsurpassed; he ranks among the best brigade and division commanders in the war. While not ideally suited to corps or army command, he performed credibly during the Atlanta Campaign; the utter failure of his Tennessee Campaign severely tarnished an otherwise stellar career.

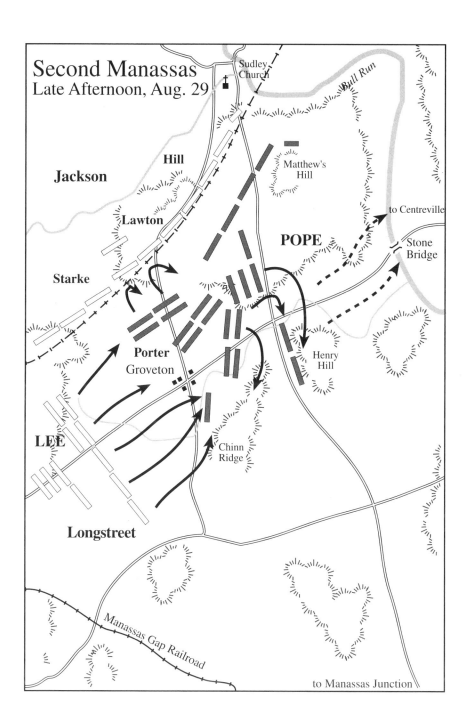

Second Manassas
Late Afternoon, Aug. 29

As the stones fell and fighting escalated along the Warrenton Turnpike, Longstreet finally launched an attack against the Federal left. He had sent General John Bell Hood's Division forward late the previous day to conduct a reconnaissance in force. Hood had achieved the biggest Confederate advance of the day and bloodied a few Union noses, but no strategic advantage had been scored. Now Longstreet's entire corps—some 25,000 screaming Confederates led by Hood's Texas Brigade—burst from the woods a half mile from Chinn Ridge. They slaughtered the two Federal brigades atop the ridge. It happened so quickly, a Yankee defender recalled, that "companies had barely time to discharge their pieces once before the rebels were almost upon them."

Volley after volley ripped through the outnumbered Federals. "The balls began to fly from the woods like hail," insisted a survivor. "It was a continual hiss, snap, whiz and sluck." Bullets tore through uniforms and human flesh, splintered canteens and rifle stocks. Men ran "like dogs." Worst hit was the 5th New York Zouaves. In ten minutes, the regiment lost nearly 300 of 500 men shot. By the time the regiment limped off the ridge, after forty minutes of combat, only 60 men remained. They had sacrificed more men in a single battle than would any other regiment in the war. Even Confederate attackers, pausing long enough to survey the regiment's gallant stand, thought it a "ghastly, horrifying spectacle."

The fighting crescendoed for another hour, until 6 P.M., in which time the Confederates suffered their own casualties. Hood's Texans paid dearly for their triumphant advance. The 5th Texas lost only half the number sacrificed by the 5th New York—a mere 225 men—but that proved to be the largest Confederate regimental loss in the battle. Blessedly, however, the fighting had all but ended. Lee had not destroyed the "miscreant," but he had whipped him, and badly. The last vestiges of fighting ended on Henry Hill, the storm center of the first battle at Manassas, and the point on which Longstreet and

Jackson converged in the twilight. As Federals retreating back down Chinn Ridge collided with Federals falling back from along the Warrenton Turnpike, Lee's men closed in on the confused, disorganized, and terribly vulnerable Army of Virginia. The Federals survived the onslaught. They held Henry Hill for an hour, until nightfall, "the succor of armies hard pressed." By 7 P.M., Pope had his battered force in retreat across Bull Run and headed for Centreville.

Pope had escaped the full wrath of Lee, but few Yankee armies would be so thoroughly beaten in the war. "We were footsore and lame," admitted a New Englander; "there was hardly a man of us who was not afflicted with diarrhea; we had filled our clothes with dust and perspiration till they were all but rotten." The army was hungry, lice infected, chafed and raw. "We were," the New Englander summarized succinctly, "demoralized and discouraged." Yet Pope, even then, failed to see—or at least acknowledge—how soundly he had been whipped. Reaching Centreville sometime around 9:30 P.M., he informed Halleck by telegraph that he had "thought it best to draw back" (not *retreat*) because his men were hungry (true) and "greatly" outnumbered (clearly untrue). "The troops are in good heart," he relayed. "The enemy is badly crippled, and we shall do well enough."

Pope had lost 16,000 men, Lee 9,000. As the victorious Confederates surveyed the scene of their titanic struggle, they could see the price both sides had paid. Thousands of corpses littered the fields. "I could have walked a quarter of a mile in almost a straight line on their dead bodies without putting a foot on the ground," asserted a Rebel artillerist of the scene in front of Jackson's entrenchments. A Federal surgeon, gathering dead and wounded from the field on September 1, witnessed a final scene of the macabre drama, as Rebels collected the spoils of battle. Union dead had been stripped of all useful clothing and accoutrements. Even the wounded, unable to defend themselves, suffered abuse, with "thugs rifling the pockets of some poor fellow who had crawled into an obscure thicket to die."

On Sunday, August 31, the heavens wept for the dead on both sides, but Lee would not allow the rain to slow his pursuit. On he came, and his coming, combined with the foul weather, seemingly awakened Pope to the reality of his situation. A Union surgeon caught a glimpse of Pope sitting in his headquarters, chin resting heavily on his chest, lost in his own "gloomy reflections." Reported the doctor, "I pitied him then. I pity him now." Keeping Halleck abreast of the situation, Pope admitted, "Our troops are...much used-up and worn-out." He needed reinforcements, stressed Pope, the reinforcements McClellan had not yet seen fit to deliver. If the Rebels continued to advance, he would give them "as desperate a fight as I can force our men to stand up to," but he warned that it was entirely possible that his army would be "destroyed."

Pope and his army escaped to Washington intact. In fact, his men displayed a good measure of grit in the most significant fighting of the withdrawal at Chantilly, or Ox Hill, on September 1, when they repulsed a larger Confederate force in a driving rainstorm. Lee had hoped to inflict more damage on Pope, but conditions conspired against him. Two days of rain slowed his army's pursuit, and most of the men, particularly in Jackson's Corps, were without rations. "My men had nothing to eat," explained Lee succinctly, "they had had nothing to eat for three days." Perhaps even more importantly, they, like the Federals, were worn out.

Pope, to his credit, had also led a competent withdrawal, although by then, few people would acknowledge it. Generals and privates, alike, cursed the man who only a month earlier had promised so much. "A more utterly unfit man than Pope has never been seen," spit General Governour Warren. Alpheus Williams confided to his daughter, "All hated him," from drummer boy on up. "Suffice it to say...that more insolence, superciliousness, ignorance, and pretentiousness were

never combined in one man." Even Pope's political friends—
largely responsible for his military position—deserted him;
Lincoln reassigned him to wage total war against Indians in
Minnesota.

Pope's Confederate adversaries took it all in stride,
although some remained undecided about the source of their
victory. One of Jackson's staff officers believed the triumph at
Manassas had been determined by the "plain, hard fighting" of
the Confederate soldier. "Don't forget," the pious Jackson cor-
rected him, "it has been won by the help of God." Lee, like-
wise, paid tribute "to Almighty God...and the valour of our
troops." Longstreet's chief of artillery, General Edward Porter
Alexander, would have cautioned both Lee and Jackson "that
the Lord helps best those who do not trust in Him for even a
row of pins,...but who appreciate the whole responsibility &
hustle for themselves accordingly." But one thing, as a
Mississippi lad expressed it, remained clear to all: "We
whipped the Yankees worse this time than they was ever
whipped before."

EPILOGUE

So ended the summer of 1862 in north-central Virginia, a summer of triumphs and tragedies, of hope and despair, a summer of stern lessons. In less than two months, the strategic situation for Yankees and Confederates in Virginia had been completely reversed. Rather than having two large, advancing armies to contend with, Lee had his own army above the Rappahannock and poised to strike. Rather than carving a destructive swath across Virginia and threatening Richmond, Northerners suddenly feared for the safety of their own capital. Alpheus Williams summed up the reversal: "A splendid army almost demoralized, millions of public property given up or destroyed, thousands of lives of our best men sacrificed for no purpose."

The Lincoln-Pope plan for waging total war had failed utterly, at least for the moment. Lincoln's instincts still told him that the Confederacy could not be defeated without undertaking some similar strategy. He still believed that the political survival of his party and his administration depended on waging what William T. Sherman would call a "hard war" of exhaustion against the Rebels. The president had learned, however, that while he might have discovered the best way to achieve those ends, he had chosen the wrong man for the job. Lincoln would continue publicly to defend Pope, but he admitted to his private secretary John Hay, "Well, John, we are whipped again, I am afraid." Ultimately, Lincoln would wage his version of total war successfully, but it would take nearly two more years of hard fighting before he found the men—Grant, Sherman, and General Philip H. Sheridan—to get it right.

The Civil War never became a total war to the extent witnessed in the twentieth century. Yankees and Confederates lacked the industrial might and terrible weapons commanded by future generations. The Civil War, unlike those future conflicts, would not be defined by widespread atrocities, high civilian casualties, or mass destruction of communities. Certainly, Federal policy, which remained flexible and adaptable to local conditions throughout the contest, never sanctioned brutal or inhumane treatment of either soldiers or civilians. But total war should not be associated with or defined by barbarous intent. Not even the bombings of Dresden or Hiroshima were thought to be barbarous by the democratic and moral nations that carried them out. The keys may be found, rather, with the exhaustion of enemy resources and morale, with destruction of the enemy's will to resist.

Abraham Lincoln called the war "a People's contest," and he understood by the summer of 1862 that Confederate armies would continue to fight so long as they were supported by the people at home. Once that support vanished, once the will of the people to wage war had been broken, the Confederate armies would wither. Nothing could better undermine civilian morale than to destroy the belief that Confederate armies were capable of shielding Southern communities from the evils of occupation. If, at the same time, Federal armies could liberate slaves, confiscate foodstuffs, cripple transportation, and destroy manufacturing, all the better. As Grant applied this for-

mula in simultaneous, multipronged thrusts into the last
strongholds of the South—most notably Virginia, Georgia, and
the Carolinas—during 1864 and 1865, he stretched the
resources and strained the confidence of the Confederate
armies and people to such an extent that Union victory became
inevitable. It was a primitive, tentative step toward modern
total war, but it marked a distinct turning point.

But for the moment, the grand Army of Virginia would be
disbanded, to be absorbed into the grander Army of the
Potomac. That would take time. The army would have to be
equipped, trained, prepared for active service. "So after all this
waste of life and money and material," lamented one New
Yorker, "we are at best where we were a year ago." The entire
Yankee nation was deeply troubled, anxious, uncertain, very
nearly desperate. The government and many soldiers had lost
faith in their generals.

All but one general, that is. The Army of the Potomac still
believed in George McClellan. Lincoln had grave doubts about
his Young Napoleon's ability to defeat Lee in the field, but not
so grave as those that shadowed his opinion of Pope. Under
normal circumstances, Lincoln would have been reluctant to
stand by Little Mac, but these were abnormal times. On the
evening of September 1, Lincoln and Halleck asked McClellan
to assume command of the combined armies and the defenses
around Washington. The following morning, they called on the
general to reaffirm their faith in him, although they carefully
worded McClellan's new commission so as to limit his command to the defense of the capital—not the undertaking of a
new campaign.

Knowing only that McClellan would again lead them, most of
the army was ecstatic. Robert Gould Shaw had been despon-
dent following the retreat from Manassas. "We shall never do
much until we get a very different army from what we have
now," he informed his father on September 2. "Until the
Government finds that it is worth their while to get competent

officers & attend themselves to the organization of the army....There is a total want of discipline & system throughout." Things would be different with McClellan, thought Shaw, for he would instil discipline and pride in the army. The "enthusiasm of the troops" for him was "great," and they would "fight under him better than under any one else." That would please Shaw. "I long for the day when we shall attack the Rebels with an overwhelming force and annihilate them," insisted the New Englander. "May I live long enough to see them running before us hacked to little pieces."

Meantime, Lee had learned a different lesson, or rather, sensed a new opportunity. His aggressive nature aside, Lee believed the North had never been more vulnerable than it was in September 1862. He had lost nearly 20 percent of his army at Second Manassas, as well as many horses, mules, and needed accoutrements. But he understood that the North was in disarray, its Eastern armies "much weakened and demoralized." On September 3, while councils in the North conferred about what was best for their army, Lee reached a decision of his own. "The present seems to be the most propitious time since the commencement of the war," he informed President Davis, "for the Confederate Army to enter Maryland." The operation entailed some risk, admitted Lee, but failure to exploit this opportunity could produce even greater risks. "[W]e cannot afford to be idle," he declared.

The next day, the Army of Northern Virginia began crossing the Potomac River. The sleepy Maryland town of Sharpsburg lay ahead. There, on September 17, Lee and McClellan would clash in the bloodiest single day of the war. The combined armies would leave 21,000 dead and wounded on the field. The battle would be a draw, but when Lee retreated below the Potomac, McClellan and Lincoln declared victory. Lincoln would seize the opportunity to issue his Emancipation Proclamation, a direct attack on Southern "property," a calculated blow to Southern morale, and a subtle means of maintaining a policy of total war.

APPENDIX A

ORDER OF BATTLE
BATTLE OF CEDAR MOUNTAIN
AUGUST 9, 1862

CONFEDERATE
THOMAS J. JACKSON, COMMANDING

RICHARD S. EWELL'S DIVISION
JUBAL A. EARLY'S BRIGADE:
13th Virginia
25th Virginia
31st Virginia
52nd Virginia
58th Virginia
12th Georgia

HENRY FORNO'S BRIGADE:
5th Louisiana
6th Louisiana
7th Louisiana
8th Louisiana
14th Louisiana

ISAAC R. TIMBLE'S BRIGADE:
15th Alabama
21st Georgia
21st North Carolina

Artillery
ALFRED R. COURTNEY
Latimer's (Va.) Battery
Dement's (Md.) Battery
Brown's (Md.) Battery [Chesapeake Artillery]
D'Aquin's (La.) Battery
Terry's (Va.) Battery [Bedford Artillery]

AMBROSE POWELL HILL'S DIVISION

LAWRENCE O. BRANCH BRIGADE:
7th North Carolina
18th North Carolina
28th North Carolina
33rd North Carolina
37th North Carolina

JAMES J. ARCHER'S BRIGADE:
1st Tennessee
7th Tennessee
14th Tennessee
5th Alabama Battalion
19th Georgia

EDWARD L. THOMAS'S BRIGADE:
14th Georgia
35th Georgia
45th Georgia
49th Georgia

MAXCY GREGG'S BRIGADE:
1st South Carolina
12th South Carolina
13th South Carolina
14th South Carolina
1st (Orr's) South Carolina Rifles

WILLIAM E. STARKE'S BRIGADE:
1st Louisiana
2nd Louisiana
9th Louisiana
10th Louisiana
15th Louisiana

CHARLES W. FIELD'S BRIGADE:
40th Virginia
47th Virginia
55th Virginia
22nd Virginia Battalion

W. DORSEY PENDER'S BRIGADE:
16th North Carolina
22nd North Carolina
34th North Carolina
38th North Carolina

Artillery
REUBEN L. WALKER
McIntosh's (S.C.) Battery [Pee Dee Artillery]
Pegram's (Va.) Battery [Purcell Artillery]
Fleet's (Va.) Battery [Middlesex Artillery]
Braxton's (Va.) Battery [Fredericksburg Artillery]
Davidson's (Va.) Battery [Letcher Artillery]
Latham's (N.C.) Battery

THOMAS J. JACKSON'S DIVISION
CHARLES S. WINDER, COMMANDING

WINDER'S DIVISION
(CHARLES A. RONALD):
2nd Virginia
4th Virginia
5th Virginia
27th Virginia
33rd Virginia

THOMAS S. GARNETT'S BRIGADE:
21st Virginia
42nd Virginia
48th Virginia
1st (Irish) Virginia Batt.

WILLIAM B. TALLIAFERRO'S BRIGADE:
10th Virginia
23rd Virginia
37th Virginia
47th Alabama
48th Alabama

ALEXANDER R. LAWTON'S BRIGADE:

13th Georgia
26th Georgia
31st Georgia
38th Georgia
60th Georgia
61st Georgia

Artillery

RICHARD S. ANDREWS

Poague's (Va.) Artillery [Rockbridge Artillery]
Carpernter's (Va.) Battery [Alleghany Artillery]
Caskie's (Va.) Battery [Hampden Artillery]

Cavalry

BEVERLY H. ROBERTSON

6th Virginia
7th Virginia
17th Virginia Battalion
2nd Virginia (detachment)
4th Virginia (detachment)
Chew's (Va.) Battery

UNION

JOHN POPE, COMMANDING

NATHANIEL P. BANK'S CORPS

ALPHEUS S. WILLIAMS'S DIVISION

SAMUEL W. CRAWFORD'S BRIGADE:
5th Connecticut
10th Maine
28th New York
46th Pennsylvania

GEORGE H. GORDON'S BRIGADE:
2nd Massachusetts
3rd Wisconsin
27th Indiana
Zoauaves d'Afrique
(Collis's Compnay)

CHRISTOPHER C. AUGUR'S DIVISION
HENRY PRICE, COMMANDING

JOHN W. GEARY'S BRIGADE:
5th Ohio
7th Ohio
29th Ohio
66th Ohio

HENRY PRICE'S BRIGADE (DAVID P. DEWITT):
3rd Maryland
102nd New York
109th Pennsylvania
111th Pennsylvania
8th & 12th U.S. Batt.

GEORGE S. GREENE'S BRIGADE:
1st District of Columbia
78th New York

Corps Artillery
CLERMONT L. BEST
4th Battery (Robinson) Maine Light Artillery
6th Battery (McGilvery) Maine Light Artillery
1st New York Light Artillery
Battery K (Crounse)
Battery L (Reynolds)
Battery M (Cothran)
2nd New York Light Artillery, Battery L (Roemer)
10th Battery (Bruen) New York Light Artillery
Pennsylvania Light Artillery, Battery K (Knap)
4th U.S. Artillery, Battery F (Howard)

IRVIN MCDOWELL'S CORPS

JAMES B. RICKETT'S DIVISION

ABRAM DURYEA'S BRIGADE:
97th New York
104th New York
105th New York
107th Pennsylvania

ZEALOUS B. TOWER'S BRIGADE:
26th New York
94th New York
88th Pennsylvania
90th Pennsylvania

GEORGE L. HARTSUFF'S BRIGADE:
11th Pennsylvania
12th Massachusetts
13th Massachusetts
83rd New York

SAMUEL S. CARROLL'S BRIGADE:
7th Indiana
84th Pennsylvania
110th Pennsylvania
1st Virginia (Union)

Corps Artillery
DAVIS TILLSON
2nd Battery (Hall) Maine Light Artillery
5th Battery (Leppien) Maine Light Artillery
1st Pennsylvania Light Artillery, Battery F (Matthews)
Pennsylvania Light Artillery, Battery C (Thompson)

Cavalry
GEORGE D. BAYARD
1st Maine
1st New Jersey
1st Pennsylvania
1st Rhode Island
1st Ohio (detachment), Pope's Escorty
1st Michigan (detachment), Banks's escort
5th New York (detachment), Banks's escort
1st Virginia (Union) (detachment), Banks's escort

APPENDIX B

ORDER OF BATTLE
BATTLE OF SECOND MANASSAS
AUGUST 28-30, 1862

CONFEDERATE
ARMY OF NORTHERN VIRGINIA
ROBERT E. LEE, COMMANDING

JAMES LONGSTREET'S CORPS

RICHARD H. ANDERSON'S DIVISION

LEWIS A. ARMISTEAD'S BRIGADE:
9th Virginia
14th Virginia
38th Virginia
53rd Virginia
57th Virginia
5th Virginia Battalion

WILLIAM MAHONE'S BRIGADE:
6th Virginia
12th Virginia
16th Virginia
41st Virginia
49th Virginia

AMBROSE R. WRIGHT'S BRIGADE:
3rd Georgia
22nd Georgia
44th Georgia
48th Georgia

DAVID R. JONES'S DIVISION

ROBERT TOOMBS'S BRIGADE (HENRY L. BENNING):
2nd Georgia
15th Georgia
17th Georgia
20th Georgia

THOMAS F. DRAYTON'S BRIGADE:
50th Georgia
51st Georgia
15th South Carolina
Phillips's Legion

JONES'S BRIGADE (GEORGE T. ANDERSON):
1st Georgia
7th Georgia
8th Georgia
9th Georgia
11th Georgia

CADMUS M. WILCOX'S DIVISION

WILCOX'S BRIGADE:
8th Alabama
9th Alabama
10th Alabama
11th Alabama
Anderson' (Va.) Battery [Thomas Artillery]

ROGER A. PRYOR'S BRIGADE:
14th Alabama
5th Florida
8th Florida
3rd Virginia

WINFIELD S. FEATHERSTON'S BRIGADE:
12th Mississippi
16th Mississippi
19th Mississippi
2nd Mississippi Battalion
Chapman's (Va.) Battery, [Dixie Artillery]

JOHN B. HOOD'S DIVISION

HOOD'S (TEXAS) BRIGADE:
18th Georgia
Hampton's (S.C.) Legion
1st Texas
4th Texas
5th Texas

WILLIAM WHITING'S BRIGADE (EVANDER M. LAW):
4th Alabama
2nd Mississippi
11th Mississippi
6th North Carolina

Artillery
BUSHROD W. FROBEL
Bachman's (S.C.) Battery [German Artillery]
Garden's (S.C.) Battery [Palmetto Artillery]
Reilly's (N.C.) Battery [Rowan Artillery]

JAMES L. KEMPER'S DIVISION

KEMPER'S BRIGADE (MONTGOMERY D. CORSE):
1st Virginia
7th Virginia
11th Virginia
17th Virginia
24th Virginia

MICAH JENKINS'S BRIGADE:
1st South Carolina
2nd South Carolina Rifles
5th South Carolina
6th South Carolina
4th South Carolina Battalion
Palmetto (S.C.) Sharpshooters

GEORGE E. PICKETT'S BRIGADE (EPPA HUNTON):
8th Virginia
18th Virginia
19th Virginia
28th Virginia
56th Virginia

NATHAN G. EVANS'S BRIGADE:
17th South Carolina
18th South Carolina
22nd South Carolina
23 South Carolina
Holcombe (S.C.) Legion
Boyce's (S.C.) Battery [Macbeth Artillery]

CORPS ARTILLERY
WASHINGTON (LA.) ARTILLERY, J.B. WALTON
Eshleman's (4th) Company
Miller's (3rd) Company
Richardson's (2nd) Company
Squires's (1st) Company

LEE'S BATTALION, STEPHEN D. LEE
Eubank's (Va.) Battery
Grimes's (Va.) Battery
Jordan's (Va.) Battery [Bedford Artillery]
Parker's (Va.) Battery
Rhett's (S.C.) Battery
Taylor's (Va.) Battery

Huger's (Va.) Battery
Leake's (Va.) Battery
Maurin's (La.) Battery [Donaldsonville Artillery]
Moorman's (Va.) Battery
Roger's (Va.) Battery [Loudon Artillery]
Stribling's (Va.) Battery [Fauquier Artillery]

THOMAS J. JACKSON'S CORPS

WILLIAM B. TALIAFERRO'S DIVISION

FIRST BRIGADE (WILLIAM S. BAYLOR):
2nd Virginia
4th Virginia
5th Virginia
27th Virginia
33rd Virginia

SECOND BRIGADE (BRADLEY T. JOHNSON):
21st Virginia
42nd Virginia
48th Virginia
1st Virginia Battalion

THIRD BRIGADE (ALEXANDER G. TALIFERRO):
47th Alabama
48th Alabama
10th Virginia
23rd Virginia
37th Virginia

FOURTH BRIGADE (WILLIAM E. STARKE):
1st Louisiana
2nd Louisiana
9th Louisiana
10th Louisiana
15th Louisiana
Coppen's (La.) Battaltion

Artillery
L.M. SHUMAKER
Brockenbrough's (Md.) Battery
Carpernter's (Va.) Battery
Caskie's (Va.) Battery [Hampden Artillery]
Cutshaw's (Va.) Battery
Poague's (Va.) Battery [Rockbridge Artillery]
Raines's (Va.) Battery [Lee Artillery]
Rice's (Va.) Battery
Wooding's (Va.) Battery [Danville Artillery]

AMBROSE POWELL HILL'S LIGHT DIVISION

LAWRENCE O. BRANCH'S BRIGADE:
7th North Carolina
18th North Carolina
28th North Carolina
33rd North Carolina
37th North Carolina

W. DORSEY PENDER'S BRIGADE:
16th North Carolina
22nd North Carolina
34th North Carolina
38th North Carolina

MAXCY GREGG'S BRIGADE:
1st South Carolina
1st South Carolina Rifles
12th South Carolina
13th South Carolina
14th South Carolina

JAMES J. ARCHER'S BRIGADE:
5th Alabama Battalion
19th Georgia
1st Tennessee
7th Tennessee
14th Tennessee

CHARLES W. FIELD'S BRIGADE:
40th Virginia
47th Virginia
55th Virginia
22nd Virginia Battalion

EDWARD L. THOMAS'S BRIGADE:
14th Georgia
35th Georgia
45th Georgia
49th Georgia

Artillery
REUBEN L. WALKER
Braxton's (Va.) Battery [Fredericksburg Artillery]
Crenshaw's (Va.) Battery
Davidson's (Va.) Battery [Letcher Artillery]
Fleet's (Va.) Battery [Middlesex Artillery]
Latham's (N.C.) Battery [Branch Artillery]
McIntosh's (S.C.) Battery [Pee Dee Artillery]
Pegram's (Va.) Battery [Purcell Artillery]

RICHARD S. EWELL'S DIVISION

ALEXANDER R. LAWTON'S BRIGADE:
13th Georgia
26th Georgia
31st Georgia
38th Georgia
60th Georgia
61st Georgia

ISAAC R. TRIMBLE'S BRIGADE:
15th Alabama
12th Georgia
21st Georgia
21st North Carolina
1st North Carolina Battalion

JUBAL A. EARLY'S BRIGADE:
13th Virginia
25th Virginia
31st Virginia
44th Virginia
49th Virginia
52nd Virginia
58th Virginia

HARRY T. HAYS'S BRIGADE (HENRY FORNO):
5th Louisiana
6th Louisiana
7th Louisiana
8th Louisiana
14th Louisiana

Artillery
Balthis's (Va.) Battery [Staunton Artillery]
Brown's (Md.) Battery [Chesapeake Artillery]
D'Aquin's Battery [Louisiana Guard Artillery]
Dement's (Md.) Battery
John R. Johnson's (Va.) Battery
Latimer's (Va.) Battery [Courtney Artillery]

Cavalry
JAMES E.B. STUART, COMMANDING

WADE HAMPTON'S BRIGADE (NOT PRESENT):
1st North Carolina
2nd South Carooina
10th Virginia
Cobb's (Ga.) Legion
Jeff Davis Legion

BEVERLY H. ROBERTSON'S BRIGADE:
2nd Virginia
6th Virginia
7th Virginia
12th Virginia
17th Virginia Battalion

FITZHUGH LEE'S BIGADE:
1st Virginia
3rd Virginia
4th Virginia
5th Virginia
9th Virginia

Artillery
Hart's (S.C.) Battery
Pelham's (Va.) Battery

UNION

ARMY OF VIRGINIA
JOHN POPE, COMMANDING

FIRST ARMY CORPS
FRANZ SIGEL, COMMANDING

FIRST DIVISION
ROBERT C. SCHENCK, COMMANDING

FIRST BRIGADE (JULIUS STAHEL):
8th New York
41st New York
45th New York
27th Pennsylvania
New York Light Artillery, 2nd Battery

SECOND BRIGADE (NATHANIEL C. MCLEAN):
25th Ohio
55th Ohio
73rd Ohio
75th Ohio
1st Ohio Light Artillery, Battery K

SECOND DIVISION
ADOLPH VON STEINWEHR, COMMANDING

FIRST BRIGADE (JOHN A. KOLTES):
29th New York
68th Pennsylvania
73rd Pennsylvania

THIRD DIVISION
CARL SHURZ, COMMANDING

FIRST BRIGADE (ALEXANDER SCHIMMELFENNING):
61st Ohio
74th Pennsylvania
8th West Virginia
Pennsylvania Light
Artillery, Battery F

SECOND BRIGADE (WLADIMIR KRZYZANOWSKI):
54th New York
58th New York
75th Pennsylvania
2nd New York Light
Artillery, Battery I

Unattached: 3rd West Virginia
Cavalry, Company C
1st Ohio Light
Artillery, Battery I

Independent Brigade
ROBERT H. MILROY, COMMANDING
82nd Ohio
2nd West Virginia
3rd West Virginia
5th West Virginia
1st West Virginia Cavalry, Companies C, E, I
Ohio Light Artillery, 12th Battery

Cavalry Brigade
JOHN BEARDSLEY, COMMANDING

1st Battalion Connecticut
1st Maryland
4th New York
9th New York
6th Ohio

Reserve Artillery

LOUIS SCHIRMER

1st New York Light Artillery, Battery I

New York Light Artillery, 13th Battery

West Virginia Light Artillery, Battery C

SECOND ARMY CORPS

NATHANIEL P. BANKS, COMMANDING

FIRST DIVISION

ALPHEUS S. WILLIAMS, COMMANDING

FIRST BRIGADE (SAMUEL W. CRAWFORD):

5th Connecticut

10th Maine

46th Pennsylvania

THIRD BRIGADE (GEORGE H. GORDON):

27th Indiana

2nd Massachusetts

3rd Wisconsin

SECOND DIVISION

GEORGE S. GREENE, COMMANDING

FIRST BRIGADE (CHARLES CANDY):

5th Ohio

7th Ohio

29th Ohio

66th Ohio

28th Pennsylvania

SECOND BRIGADE (M. SCHLAUDECKER):

3rd Maryland

102nd New York

109th Pennsylvania

111th Pennsylvania

8th & 12th U.S. Battalion

THIRD BRIGADE (JAMES A. TAIT):
3rd Delaware
1st District of Columbia
60th New York
78th New York
Purnell Legion, Maryland

Artillery
CLERMONT L. BEST, COMMANDING
Maine Light Artillery
4th Battery
6th Battery
1st New York Light Artillery, Battery M
New York Light Artillery, 10th Battery
Pennsylvania Light Artillery, Battery E
4th U.S. Artillery, Battery F

Cavalry Brigade
JOHN BUFORD, COMMANDING
1st Michigan
5th New York
1st Vermont
1st West Virginia

THIRD ARMY CORPS
IRVIN MCDOWELL, COMMANDING

FIRST DIVISION
RUFUS KING, COMMANDING

FIRST BRIGADE (JOHN P. HATCH):
22nd New York
24th New York
30th New York
84th New York (14th Militia)
2nd U.S. Sharpshooters

SECOND BRIGADE (ABNER DOUBLEDAY):
76th New York
95th New York
56th Pennsylvania

THIRD BRIGADE (MARSENA R. PATRICK):
21st New York
23rd New York
35th New York
80th New York (20th Militia)

FOURTH BRIGADE (JOHN GIBBON):
19th Indiana
2nd Wisconsin
6th Wisconsin
7th Wisconsin

Artillery
JOSEPH B. CAMPBELL
New Hampshire Light Artillery, 1st Battery
1st New York Light Artillery, Battery L
1st Rhode Island Light Artillery, Battery D
4th U.S. Artillery, Battery B

SECOND DIVISION
JAMES B. RICKETTS, COMMANDING

FIRST BRIGADE (ABRAM DURYEE):
97th New York
104th New York
105th New York
107th Pennsylvania

SECOND BRIGADE (ZEALOUS B. TOWER):
26th New York
94th New York
88th Pennsylvania
90th Pennsylvania

THIRD BRIGADE (ROBERT STILES):
12th Massachusetts
13th Massachusetts
83rd New York (9th Militia)
11th Pennsylvania

FOURTH BRIGADE (JOSEPH THOBURN):
7th Indiana
84th Pennsylvania
1st West Virginia

Artillery
Maine Light Artillery
2nd Battery
5th Battery
1st Pennsylvania Light Artillery, Battery F
Pennsylvania Light Artillery, Battery C

Cavalry Brigade
GEORGE D. BAYARD, COMMANDING
1st Maine
1st New Jersey
2nd New York
1st Pennsylvania
1st Rhode Island

Unattached
Indiana Light Artillery, 16th Battery
3rd Indiana Cavaly (detachment)
4th U.S. Artillery, Battery E

PENNSYLVANIA RESERVES
JOHN F. REYNOLDS, COMMANDING

FIRST BRIGADE (GEORGE G. MEADE):
3rd Pennsylvania Reserves
4th Pennsylvania Reserves
7th Pennsylvania Reserves
8th Pennsylvania Reserves
13th Pennsylvania Reserves (1st Rifles)

SECOND BRIGADE (THURMAN SEYMOUR):
1st Pennsylvania Reserves
2nd Pennsylvania Reserves
5th Pennsylvania Reserves
6th Pennsylvania Reserves

THIRD BRIGADE (CONRAD F. JACKSON):
9th Pennsylvania Reserves
10th Pennsylvania Reserves
11th Pennsylvania Reserves
12th Pennsylvania Reserves

Artillery
DUNBAR R. RANSOM
1st Pennsylvania Light Artillery
Battery A
Battery B
Battery G
5th U.S. Artillery, Battery C

RESERVES CORPS
SAMUEL D. STURGIS, COMMANDING

A. SANDERS PIATT'S BRIGADE:
63rd Indiana, Companies A, B. C. D
86th New York

ARMY OF THE POTOMAC

THIRD ARMY CORPS
SAMUEL P. HEINTZELMAN

FIRST DIVISION
PHILIP KEARNY

FIRST BRIGADE (JOHN C. ROBINSON):
20th Indiana
63rd Pennsylvania
105th Pennsylvania

SECOND BRIGADE (DAVID B. BIRNEY):
3rd Maine
4th Maine
1st New York
38th New York
40th New York
101st New York
57th Pennsylvania

THIRD BRIGADE (ORLANDO M. POE):
2nd Michigan
3rd Michigan
5th Michigan
37th New York
99th Pennsylvania

Artillery
1st Rhode Island Light Artillery, Battery E
1st U.S. Artillery, Battery K

SECOND DIVISION
JOSEPH HOOKER, COMMANDING

FIRST BRIGADE (CUVIER GROVER):
1st Massachusetts
11th Massachusetts
16th Massachusetts
2nd New Hampshire
26th Pennsylvania

SECOND BRIGADE (NELSON TAYLOR):
70th New York
71st New York
72nd New York
73rd New York
74th New York

THIRD BRIGADE (JOSEPH B. CARR):
5th New Jersey
6th New Jersey
7th New Jersey
8th New Jersey
2nd New York
115th Pennsylvania

FIFTH ARMY CORPS
GEORGE W. MORELL

FIRST BRIGADE (CHARLES W. ROBERTS):
2nd Maine
18th Massachusetts
22nd Massachusetts
1st Michigan
13th New York
25th New York

SECOND BRIGADE (CHARLES GRIFFIN):
9th Massachusetts
32nd Massachusetts
4th Michigan
14th New York
62nd Pennsylvania

THIRD BRIGADE (DANIEL BUTTERFIELD):
16th Michigan
Michigan Sharpshooters (Brady's Company)
12th New York
17th New York
44th New York
83rd Pennsylvania

Sharpshooters:
1st U.S.

Artillery
Massachusetts Light Artillery, 3rd Battery (C)
1st Rhode Island Light Artillery, Battery C
5th U.S. Artillery, Battery D

SECOND DIVISION
GEORGE SYKES

FIRST BRIGADE (ROBERT C. BUCHANAN):
3rd U.S.
4th U.S.
12th U.S., 1st Battalion
14th U.S., 1st Battalion
14th U.S., 2nd Battalion

SECOND BRIGADE (WILLIAM CHAPMAN):
1st U.S., Company G
2nd U.S.
6th U.S.
10th U.S.
11th U.S.
17th U.S.

THIRD BRIGADE (GOUVERNEUR K. WARREN):
5th New York
10th New York

Artillery
STEPHEN H. WEED
1st U.S. Artillery
Battery E
Battery G
5th U.S. Artillery
Battery I
Battery K

SIXTH ARMY CORPS

FIRST DIVISION

FIRST BRIGADE (GEORGE W. TAYLOR):
1st New Jersey
2nd New Jersey
3rd New Jersey
4th New Jersey

NINTH ARMY CORPS

FIRST DIVISION
ISAAC I. STEVENS, COMMANDING

FIRST BRIGADE (BENJAMIN C. CHRIST):
8th Michigan
50th Pennsylvania

SECOND BRIGADE (DANIEL LEASURE):
46th New York
100th Pennsylvania

THIRD BRIGADE (ADDISON FARNSWORTH):
28th Massachusetts
79th New York

Artillery
Massachusetts Light Artillery, 8th Battery
2nd U.S. Artillery, Battery E

SECOND DIVISION
JESSE L. RENO

FIRST BRIGADE (JAMES NAGLE):
2nd Maryland
6th New Hampshire
48th Pennsylvania

SECOND BRIGADE (EDWARD FERRERO):
21st Massachusetts
51st New York
51st Pennsylvania

KANAWHA DIVISION (DETACHMENT)
E. PARKER SCAMMON, COMMANDING
11th Ohio
12th Ohio
30th Ohio
36th Ohio

FURTHER READING

Ash, Stephen V. *When the Yankees Came: Conflict and Chaos in the Occupied South, 1861–1865.* Chapel Hill: University of North Carolina Press, 1995.

Beale, Howard K. ed. *Diary of Gideon Welles.* 3 vols. New York: W.W. Norton, 1960.

Buck, Samual D. *With the Old Confederates: Actual Experiences of a Captain in the Line.* Gaithersburg, Md.: Butternut Press, 1983.

Blackford, Susan Leigh, comp. *Letters from Lee's Army.* New York: Charles Scribner's Sons, 1947.

Donald, David H. *Lincoln.* New York: Simon & Schuster, 1995.

Douglas, Henry Kyd. *I Rode with Stonewall.* Chapel Hill: University of North Carolina Press, 1940.

Duncan, Russell, ed. *Blue-Eyed Child of Fortune: The Civil War Letters of Colonel Robert Gould Shaw.* Athens: University of Georgia Press, 1992.

Eby, Cecil D., Jr., ed. *A Virginia Yankee in the Civil War: The Diaries of David Hunter Strother.* Chapel Hill: University of North Carolina Press, 1961.

Engle, Stephen D. *Yankee Dutchman: The Life of Franz Sigel.* Fayetteville: University of Arkansas Press, 1993.

Gallagher, Gary W., ed. *Fighting for the Confederacy: The Personal Recollections of General Edward Porter Alexander.* Chapel Hill: University of North Carolina Press, 1989.

Grimsley, Mark. *The Hard Hand of War: Union Military Policy toward Southern Civilians, 1861–1865.* Cambridge: Cambridge University Press, 1995.

Harrington, Fred H. *Fighting Politician: Major General N.P. Banks.* Philadlephia: Pennsylvania University Press, 1948.

Henderson, G.F.R. *Stonewall Jackson and the American Civil War.* New York: Grosset & Dunlap, 1949.

Hennessy, John J. *Return to Bull Run: The Campaign and Battle of Second Manassas.* New York: Simon & Schuster, 1993.

Hotchkiss, Jedediah. *Make Me a Map of the Valley: The Civil War Journal of Stonewall Jackson's Topographer.* Ed. Archie P. McDonald. Dallas: Southern Methodist University Press, 1973.

Krick, Robert K. *Stonewall Jackson at Cedar Mountain.* Chapel Hill: University of North Carolina Press, 1990.

Oates, Stephen B. *A Woman of Valor: Clara Barton and the Civil War.* New York: The Free Press, 1994.

Quaife, Milo M., ed. *From the Cannon's Mouth: The Civil War Letters of General Alpheus S. Williams.* Detroit: Wayne State University Press, 1959.

Robertson, James I., Jr. *General A.P. Hill: The Story of a Confederate Warrior.* New York: Random House, 1987.

Ropes, John C. *The Army Under Pope.* New York: Charles Scribner's Sons, 1881.

Royster, Charles. *The Destructive War: William Tecumseh Sherman, Stonewall Jackson, and the Americans.* New York: 1991.

Schutz, Wallace J. and Walter N. Trenerry. *Abandoned by Lincoln: A Military Biography of General John Pope.* Urbana: University of Illinois Press, 1990.

Sears, Stephen W. *George B. McClellan: The Young Napoleon.* New York: Ticknor & Fields, 1988.

Sparks, David S., ed. *Inside Lincoln's Army: The Diary of Marsena Rudolph Patrick, Provost Marshal, Army of the Potomac.* New York: Thomas Yoseloff, 1964.

Stackpole, Edward J. *From Cedar Mountain to Antietam.* Harrisburg, Pa.: Stackpole Books, 1959.

Sutherland, Daniel E. *Seasons of War: The Ordeal of a Confederate Community, 1861–1865.* New York: The Free Press, 1995.

Swinton, William. *Campaigns of the Army of the Potomac.* New York: Charles Scribner's Sons, 1882.

Thomas, Emory M. *Bold Dragoon: The Life of J.E.B. Stuart.* New York: Harper & Row, 1986.

Thomas, Emory M. *Robert E. Lee: A Biography.* New York: W. W. Norton, 1995.

Townsend, George Alfred. *Campaigns of a Non-Combatant.* New York: Time-Life Books, 1982.

Wert, Jeffry D. *General James Longstreet: The Confederacy's Most Controversial Soldier.* New York: Simon & Schuster, 1993.

PHOTO CREDITS

We acknowledge the cooperation of the U.S. Army Military History Institute at Carlisle Barracks, Pennsylvania for the photographs of Nathaniel P. Banks, Clarissa Harlowe Barton, Samuel W. Crawford, Jubal A. Early, Henry W. Halleck, Ambrose Powell Hill, John Bell Hood, Thomas J. Jackson, Philip Kearny, Rufus King, Abraham Lincoln , Fitz John Porter, Robert Gould Shaw, Franz Sigel, William B. Taliaferro, Isaac R. Trimble, and Alpheus S. Williams.

We credit the Library of Congress for the photographs of Richard S. Ewell, Robert E. Lee, James Longstreet, James E.B. Stuart, black refugees fleeing with Pope's army, Culpeper Court House, and horses felled on the battlefield at Cedar Mountain.

The photograph of John Pope is from the National Archives.

The view of the Battle of Cedar Mountain is from *Leslie's Illustrated Newspaper.*

INDEX

Alexander, Edward P., 87
Alexandria, Va., 67
Andrews, Richard S., 42
Army of Northern Virginia, 91
Army of the Potomac, 20–21, 53, 66, 68–69, 77, 78, 90
Army of Virginia, 15 21–22, 55, 81, 85, 90
Augur, Christopher C., 37

Banks, Nathaniel P., 21, 35, 37, 47
Barton, Clarissa H., 53–54
Bayard, George D., 59
Berry Hill, 25–26
Black troops, 14–15
Blacks, free, 27–28
Brandy Station, Va., 59, 61
Bristoe Station, Va., 64, 66
Burnside, Ambrose, 55

Casualties, 45–46, 48, 49, 50, 53, 66, 73, 80, 84, 85–86
Catlett's Station raid, 63, 65
Cedar Mountain, 37, 39; battle of, 33–49, 73
Cedar Run, 48–49, 50–51
Cedar Creek, 63
Centreville, Va., 71, 85
Chantilly, battle of, 86
Chicago *Tribune*, 21
Chinn Ridge, 84–85
Civilians, during battle, 42–43; treatment of, 19–20, 21–22, 23–31, 55, 60
Clark Mountain, 57
Connecticut troops: 5th Infantry, 45
Crawford, Samuel W., 42–44, 45
Crittenden, Catherine, 38

Culpeper Road, 37, 38, 45, 47–48
Culpeper, Va., 21 25–26, 28–29, 30–31, 33, 53, 55 59–60

Davis, Jefferson, 30, 91
Dunn, James. 53

Early, Jubal A., 37–39, 80
Eastern Theater, 14, 20–21
Emanicipation, 14, 20, 91
Ewell, Richard S., 33–34, 38, 67–68

Forest Grove, 42
Fredericksburg, Va., 21, 33, 37, 55
Fremont, John, 19, 20

Geary, John W., 37
Georgia troops: 21st Infantry, 73; 26th Infantry, 73
Gordon, George H., 46
Gordonsville, Va., 31, 55
Gorrell, Joseph, 59–60
Grant, Ulysses S., 16, 89–90
Greene, George S., 37
Guerrillas, 19–20, 29–30

Halleck, Henry W., 16–17, 53, 67, 85, 90
Hart's Mill, 63
Hartsuff, George L., 50–51
Hatch, John P., 21
Hay, John, 89
Henry Hill, 84–85
Hill, Ambrose P., 31–33, 37, 45, 48, 80
Hinson's Mill, 63
Hood, John B., 82–84
Hooker, Joseph, 66
Howard, McHenry, 39, 42

Indiana troops: 19th Infantry, 73

Jackson, Thomas J., 30–31, 33, 44–45, 48, 50, 58–59, 60–61,
    63–66, 67–68, 71, 73, 75, 80, 85, 87
James River, 62
Journalists, 26–27, 60

Karge, Joseph, 59
Kearny, Philip, 68–69, 75
Kelly's Ford, 59, 60, 61
Kettle Run, 66
Kilpatrick, Judson, 59
King, Rufus, 69, 71

Lee, Fitzhugh, 59
Lee, Robert E., 21, 30–31, 55–59, 60–63, 75–76, 86–87, 91
Lincoln, Abraham, 13–15, 20, 21, 22, 87, 88–89, 90, 91
Little Washington, Va., 21
Longstreet, James, 55, 58–59, 60–61, 75–76, 84
Louisiana troops: 81

Maine troops: 10th Infantry, 45
Manassas, Va., 65–67, 68–69, 71
Manassas, 2nd battle of, 71–85
Massachusetts troops: generally, 56; 2d Infantry, 45–47
McClellan, George B., 13–14, 21, 55, 66–67, 78, 90–91
McDowell, Irvin, 21, 33, 71
Mississippi troops: 87
Missouri, 19–20

Nalle, William, 42–43
New York troops: generally, 71–72, 81; 2d Cavalry, 59; 28th
    Infantry, 45; 76th Infantry, 73; 5th Zouaves, 84
New Jersey troops: 1st Cavalry, 25, 59
North Carolina troops, 47

Orange & Alexandria Railroad, 53, 63
Orange County, Va., 55

Peninsula, 55, 59; campaign, 14
Pennsylvania troops: 1st Cavalry, 47–48; 46th Infantry, 45;
    56th Infantry, 73
Phelps, John, 22
Pope, John, 16–20, 21–22, 31, 33, 37, 47, 50, 53, 63–64, 67,
    71, 75, 77–81, 85–86; his general orders, 21–23, 25, 55
Porter, Fitz John, 77–79
Press, northern, 14, 21
Prince, Henry, 37

Raccoon Ford, 59
Radical Republicans, 14
Rapidan River, 31, 33, 51, 53, 55, 57, 59
Rappahannock River, 21, 48, 53, 55–56, 59, 61, 63, 64, 88;
    bridge, 61
Rebel yell, 73
Reno, Jesse, 55
Richmond, Va., 30, 62, 88
Roberts, Benjamin S., 50–51
Robertson, Beverly, 59

Seven Days' Battles, 21, 59
Seward, William, 14
Sharpsburg, battle of, 91
Shaw, Robert G., 46, 51, 90–91
Shenandoah Valley, 16, 21
Sheridan, Philip H., 89
Sherman, William T., 19, 89
Sigel, Franz, 21, 36–37, 48, 75
Slaughter, Philp, 38
Slaves, 14–15, 25–26, 27–28
Somerville Ford, 59

Sperryville, Va., 21
Stanton, Edwin, 22
Starke, William E., 81
Stevens, Isaac I., 55
Stevensburg, Va., 59, 60–61
Strategy, Confederate, 30–31, 51, 55–56, 61–64, 88, 91;
    Federal, 14–15, 20, 21–22, 55–56, 67, 88–89
Stuart, James E. B., 50–52, 61–63
Sulpher Springs, Va., 63

Taliaferro, William B., 41, 43–44
Texas troops: Texas Brigade, 84; 5th Infantry, 84
Thom, Lucy, 25–26
Thoroughfare Gap, 63–64, 75–76
Total war, 13–14, 15, 88–90, 91
Trans-Mississippi Theater, 14, 20
Trimble, Isaac I., 72–73

Virginia troops: generally, 47; Richmond Howitzers, 60;
    Stonewall Brigade, 44, 73; 13th Infantry, 37–38, 47–48;
    21st Infantry, 62

Walker, James A., 37–38, 47
Warren, Governour, 86
Warrenton Turnpike, 71, 84–85
Warrenton, Va., 21
Washington, D.C., 16, 67, 86, 90
Waterloo, Va., 63; bridge, 63
Welles, Gideon, 14
Western Theater, 14, 21
Williams, Alpheus, 43, 47, 86, 88
Winder, Charles S., 33, 37, 38–39, 42
Wisconsin troops: generally, 71, 73; 2nd Wisconsin Infantry,
    73; 3rd Infantry, 45
Women, treatment of, 25–27, 28